# Authority, Creativity and the Third Imperium

## Why God's Knowing Himself, Outside Himself, Matters

Sean J. O'Reilly

House of a Thousand Suns
Publishing for a New Age
131 East Main Street
Suite A
Front Royal, VA  22630

Cover Image by Amazon KDP
ISBN: 1507668546
ISBN 13: 9781507668542
Non-Fiction
Categories:
Body, Mind and Spirit
Philosophy
Political Science
Social Studies

SOL·ISANCTISSIMOSACRVM

The picture above, the head surrounded by a radiant crown or nimbus, is a detail from a marble altar dedicated to the Sun god. From Palmyra (Syria), it dates from the second half of the first century AD and now is in the Galleria Lapidaria (Capitoline Museums, Rome). The first line reads "Sacred to the most holy Sun." The eagle was thought to be the messenger of the god.[1]

---

[1] Source: (penelope.uchicago.edu/~grout/.../invictus.html University of Chicago)

*"For political ideas acquire operative force in human affairs when, as we have seen, they acquire legitimacy, when they have the title of being right which binds men's consciences. Then they possess, as the Confucian doctrine has it, "the mandate of heaven."* [2]

---

[2] Lippmann, Walter, *The Public Philosophy*, copyright 1956 by Mentor Books, page 138

# Table of Contents

# I

# Authority, Creativity, Virtue

# And the State

"Not to know what happened before you were born is to be a child forever. For what is the time of a man, except it be interwoven with that memory of ancient things of a superior age."

-Cicero, *Orator Ad M. Brutum* (46 BC)

## On Authority, Creativity and Politics

*"The empires of the future are the empires of the mind."*

-Churchill, speaking at Harvard University

The relationship of time to eternity is, perhaps, one of the oldest mysteries of mankind. Time is the province of humanity and eternity the realm of the Divine. The imputed intersection between the two is the basis for much of human history. Authority and politics are rooted derivatively, through invocation and claim, by culture and civilization in this same mystery. The mythical claim of rule by divine right or dispensation, for example, is so old that its origins are lost to us. The ancient Egyptians saw the Pharaoh as the representative of God on earth. This was followed by the divine right of kings in Europe, which claimed that a monarch was subject to no earthly authority, deriving the right to rule directly from the will of God. Even now, moral claims are politically invoked by Jews, Christians, Muslims and other groups using religious principles given by divine law as their intellectual axis or basis for action.

The role of creativity in interpreting these different layers of authority and mystery is paramount in order to better understand both culture and politics. Mythical correlatives are not necessarily congruent with causality, so the importance of distinguishing between science and assertions based on older forms of knowledge has become more important than ever before.

Myth, by all accounts, attempts to penetrate the veil of time by hinting at things that tremble at the edge of imagination and memory. According to Greek mythology, Astraea, the celestial virgin, was the last of the immortals to live with humans during the Golden Age, which was one of the five declining Ages of Man. The Roman poet Ovid, claimed that Astraea abandoned the earth during the Iron Age due to mans' inhumanity to man. She ascended to heaven to become the constellation Virgo, where she holds the scales of justice. This is a beautiful, but only correlative assertion between myth and history, and like many religious or quasi-religious correlations, not a scientific fact.

The Greek poet Hesiod, in his *Works and Days*, dated to approximately 700 BC, described the decline of mankind, from its' original association with the Gods through various ages: from a golden age ruled by Chronos, the God of Time, to a silver age ruled by mothers, to a bronze age ruled by war and then to an iron age characterized by human misery. Each age was followed by a leaden age of decline. The heroic or sixth age was one that improved any age that it preceded. In the golden age, humans mingled freely with the Gods and were without flaw. The earth was abundant, man did not have to work and knew no master.[3] There is a rough similarity of this myth to the biblical Garden of Eden but almost all cultures have myths of a golden age, which is followed by cycles of decline and rejuvenation.

---

[3] *How the Golden Age Lost Its Memory* by Andrew Heisel, Los Angeles Book Review, March 22, 2015

J.R.R. Tolkien, in more recent times, created an entire mythology that hinted at rich histories that never existed except, perhaps, in the power of mind. Who can read, for example, about the fall of Númenor and the founding of Gondor by the men of the West without feeling that some lost truth is being grasped or hinted at? However conceived, the golden age is always in the past and its job is to remind us how much better things could be.⁴ It is the purpose of this book to show how life could be made politically and economically better for all of us, by more clearly understanding the relationship of time to eternity, and the creative principles upon which America was founded.

The hope of a return to a golden age, a recurring theme throughout history, was noted by the Roman poet Virgil in 44 B.C.

*"Now the last age by [the] Sibyl sung*
*Has come and gone, and the majestic roll*
*Of circling centuries begins anew:*
*Astraea returns,*
*Returns old Saturn's reign,*
*With a new breed of men sent down from heaven."* ⁵

Our present age might be characterized as a leaden age in which almost forms of authority are subject to doubt. Science, in the form of absolute certainty about the observable and the provable, has cast a shadow of uncertainty on the unseen and the hidden, which is the province of morality, religion and the

---

⁴ Ibid
⁵ *The Eclogue*, Virgil, 44-38 BC. The Sibyl was a temple prophetess.

storied realms of the heroic and the mythical. Given the historically demonstrable power of the unseen, in terms of belief and intuition, the enterprise of reconstituting the priority of this hidden world by "a new breed of men" and women takes on a special urgency. How can we possibly understand the motivations of the great sages and political leaders throughout the ages and even those who seem to have been motivated by a darkness so great that even today we shudder? The relationship between authority, creativity and the political order is, as this book will attempt to show, the missing link between the past, present and future direction of history.

History might be thought of, in the broadest sense, as both a written record and a reflection of the hidden face of human motivation. The historian, besides simply chronicling events, attempts to understand the impulses that roil beneath the surface of time and the various expressions of authority and intuition that harness or destroy human potential. We attribute benevolence to civilizations that build society and gaze, for the most part, with undisguised contempt at those cultures that simply exist to loot and burn.

The Pyramids, as we know today, were essentially public works projects, designed by Egyptian authorities to express the purpose and direction of a society with a complex belief system. The image of armies of slaves and overseers with whips is pure Hollywood. The reality is that we have records of worker strikes recovered from sites near the Pyramids.[6] Slaves do not engage in labor negotiations.

The images that we have of the past are often so distorted by the lens of the present that we tend to forget that human beings face the same fundamental choices and questions generation after generation: how best to move forward into the future or, what is desirable quickly attainable, or must it be worked towards by parsing time and effort? The dichotomy and struggle between what might be called the creative impulse to benevolence and self-restraint and the immediate and destructive default position of the human psyche, to appetite and fear, is also as old as history itself.

Authority, expressed in both dictatorship and civil governance, toils with and against various moral imperatives expressed in the impulse towards democracy or rule by the people. Adding further to this force, running like a river of discontent through most societies, are religious beliefs that compel legions of believers using the unspoken algorithms of fear and hope in the search for eternal life.

What is the relationship between authority, creativity and politics? Is it simply a recognition of potential, and the power to persuade or coerce, or is it a testament to a relationship between the visible world of hard data and an invisible world of inspiration and power just beyond the edge of mind? The Greek

---

[6] Multiple sources but one good reference is:
http://harvardmagazine.com/2003/07/who-built-the-pyramids-html

word "kratos" means power. A series of "oughts" and "shoulds" bursting with kratos is often generated in human discourse, just beyond the calculations of physical cause and effect, when authority, creativity and politics meet.

And where does "ought and "should" meet today? Unfortunately they don't often meet at the usual institutional junctures of politics and society. People are often left scratching their heads at the mindless repetition of slogans by politicians, and even religious leaders, who clearly have no new solutions or creative ideas to offer for pressing institutional or social issues requiring immediate attention.

Creativity is now, largely, a creature of individual and corporate enterprise and not something we attribute to politics. Politicians of all stripes tend to be mired in the accretions of legacy-driven politics and dog-whistle sloganeering. The notion of "ought," despite the dismal political and judicial scene, seems hard-wired into human consciousness, even though its interpretations vary greatly. It is no stretch to say that how we conceive of "ought," either politically, philosophically or scientifically and *how it is prioritized* is at the root of many creative decisions, both personal and political. Do we arouse our sense of creativity to engage the moral imperative of "ought", or do we engage our appetites to suppress the notion of "ought"?

There is a dark side, however, even beyond misuse of creativity: it is the non-use of creativity. As Carl Jung noted: "One of the most destructive forces is unused creative power. If a man out of laziness does not use his creative energy, his psychic energy turns to sheer poison." It is, perhaps more accurate to say, as

13

Walter Lippmann noted in his book, *The Public Philosophy*, that "when reason no longer represents society within the human psyche, then it becomes the instrument of appetite." Any society that assumes appetites are naturally self-ordering without adverting to moral standards, as a road map for good behavior, is sowing the seeds of civic discord.

Another way of mapping the dark and other problems related to intellectual and moral ignorance is to look at what happens when the mind is not presented with or given the necessary facts about human transformation and growth. The physicist Edward Teller, who was one of the fathers of the atomic bomb, stated that:

"The extinction of the human race will come from its inability to emotionally comprehend the exponential function."

Geometric growth has a constant rate of change, i.e., the increases per time period are constant. Here's an example, with a constant delta of 1:
1, 2, 3, 4, 5, 6, ...

Exponential growth is where the rate of change is itself increasing. In this example, each number is double the previous one:
1, 2, 4, 8, 16, ...

The notion that whenever we act or choose, we step onto a stage where the floor itself can change under us, is worth reflecting on. Scientists tend to apply this exponential function to the degradation of nature caused by environmental pollution or the exponential consumption created by a high birth rate. There is, however, another meaning. What this also means is that when the notion of creativity and the moral imperative of "ought" are understood *as an exponential function* produced by a relationship or ratio between ourselves and what might be called a Higher Power (no pun intended) then the limits to what we can do or even ought to do cannot be understood simply as a linear progression within a given set of rules. Rules are what occur, so to speak, in the rear view mirror of consciousness. This doesn't obviate the value of rules; it just means they are subject to a higher power.

**Authority, Creativity and Identity**

Authority is defined as: "the power or right to give orders, make decisions, and enforce obedience." This is what we commonly think about when we refer to political power. Creativity, however, is defined as "the ability to transcend traditional ideas, rules, patterns, relationships, or the like, and to create meaningful new concepts, forms, methods, interpretations, etc." Authority seems linked to creativity, in the individual, as a certain power needed *to initiate* the creative process. The more authority we elect, the more power it would seem, is available (theoretically at least) for creativity. Someone who is able to rise above convention and put creative ideas into practice, in new ways, has elected or connected in some deeper way with an inner authority that is hard to "place" and even harder to adequately describe.

Authority and creativity also seem closely linked to identity. If identity is defined as a person's conception and expression of their individuality or group affiliations (such as national identity and cultural identity) then identity is as ephemeral as the wind. However, if personal identity extends beyond the local influence of personal ego, history and context into the realm of self or spiritual identity, then a host of other considerations come into play. If identity is conceived of as being related to a higher spiritual form, or soul, then the way we experience this *blended identity* of ego, self and soul may become a critical component in the subjective experience of both authority and creativity. Any proposed link between ego, soul and self or even God and the human soul, however adequately or inadequately articulated, ultimately requires a leap into metaphysics.[7]

*Accessing our identity connects us with a hidden power.*

Whether this opening to the power of identity is simply uncreated energy, as the physicists conceive of it, or is something more closely related to spirit is, in a way, unimportant for the purpose of the present investigation. Whatever it is, "it" seems to be the source of an additional, exponential power to create or to be creative that is accessible by all, in varying degrees, depending on circumstance. What is even more interesting is that when we notice the *upshift* to this place of additional power and clarity, we feel hopeful and excited. What may have seemed impossible prior to this access now seems effortless. We can do it—whatever "it" happens to be and suddenly a way forward takes shape in the inner consciousness. The glistening ship of possibility emerges slowly

_____

[7] There have been many books published on the relationship between ego and self, self and soul, and creativity and self but for the present purpose it only has to be noted as a wide field for further exploration.

from the grey fog of potential, gold coins scattered on deck and a full head of billowing, white canvas.

As an observation, it seems that whenever this kind of individual authority increases, the potential for creativity can also increase. Conversely, when political authority increases, creativity seems to decrease or become more restricted. This is painting with a broad brush but the creativity of societies that are "free" is often contrasted with the slow development of societies that are less free. The obvious question, which is seldom asked, is: How can the relationship between authority and creativity be enhanced by political systems and how is it hindered by them?

Many of the debates, for example, between liberals and conservatives in America revolve around the way the authority of the Constitution is interpreted. Rather than returning to the intent of the Founding Fathers and focusing on the meaning and origin of authority, there are those who latch onto the literal meaning of the document, seeking to extract every possible concession for the emancipation of their appetites from reason and good sense. This is often no less true of conservatives than it is of liberals. Who could read into the Constitution the "right" to loot and pillage your neighbors financially and economically under the guise of free enterprise? Conversely, who could possibly read a right to the murder of infants in the Constitution under the rubric of "choice"?

It is interesting to note that in 1776, "The Founders DID NOT establish the Constitution for the purpose of granting rights. Rather, they established this government of laws (not a government of men) in order to **secure** each person's Creator endowed rights to life, liberty, and property." [8]

This is not an irrelevant distinction as the clamor for additional "rights" continues unabated though litigation and popular appeal. When we consider that the rights guaranteed by the Constitution are Creator-endowed rights, some of the rights now sought appear not to be rights at all but only wishes.

*"Only in America, did a nation's founders recognize that rights, though endowed by the Creator as unalienable prerogatives, would not be sustained in society unless they were protected under a code of law which was itself in harmony with a higher law. They called it "natural law," or "Nature's law." Such law is the ultimate source and established limit for all of man's laws and is intended to protect each of these natural rights for all of mankind. The Declaration of Independence of 1776 established the premise that in America a people might assume the station "to which the laws of Nature and Nature's God entitle them."* [9]

"Herein lay the security for men's individual rights—an immutable code of law, sanctioned by the Creator of man's rights, and designed to promote, preserve, and protect him and his fellows in the enjoyment of their rights. They believed that such natural law, revealed to man through his reason, was capable of being understood by both the ploughman and the professor."[10]

---

[8] Natural Law:  http://www.nccs.net/natural-law-the-ultimate-source-of-constitutional-law.php
[9] Ibid
[10] Ibid

## Is Separation of Church and State Based on a False Premise?

Consequently, and in the light of the foregoing, we can suggest that the strident separation of Church and State in the United States is based on a false premise: that what God wants is somehow other than what we should want. The problem is based on something very simple. The eternal perspective of the God of religion is not the same as ours. For those of us who are not inhabiting eternity, we have different ways of thinking about God because we were never given an original, religious instruction manual.

There are many people who think the only book of instruction should be the Vedas, the Bible, the Koran or some other holy work. In order to keep people from fighting over whose instruction manual is best, the founders of America were in unanimous agreement on one thing. In the absence of proof, it is better to let everyone believe what they want to believe about God and keep the state from taking sides. This is, essentially, the tongue-in-cheek version of the separation of Church and State, as we know it, in America. We all get to have an opinion about God and His handiwork in this system, and from an extreme point of view, God may have a lot to answer for.

Who in their right minds would allow natural disasters, excrement, mosquitoes, disease, birth defects and war and famine to be part of the parade? Despite this irreverent question, the point is that we don't see things the way God does and He doesn't see things the way we do. As Paul William Roberts noted in an astonishing moment of clarity, as he was galloping on a white horse before the Pyramids at dawn, *man is more moral than God.*[11] As shocking as this sounds, it may well be true but it can only be understood by examining the origin of different perspectives. Our limited moral consciousness is based on the kinds of causality we see and understand in time. God's moral perspective is based on a completely different, infinite and eternal consciousness.

If we step outside the box for a moment, our perspective and God's can be seen as two different and complementary points of view. God seems to cut us a great deal of slack because we don't have the perspective afforded by eternity. Perhaps we should do the same for Him. Part of having free will, and not just paying lip service to the concept, is that we actually don't have to agree with God and He won't force the issue; He will, however, keep on doing what it is that He does until we get it. God will not lose any sleep over our disobedience. He knew about the problems from the very beginning and He still thought it was all good.

There is, in the New Testament, (and this is said with equal amounts of humor, respect, horror and caution) a kind of crankiness that we might ascribe to Jesus and his milieu. You know, things like plucking your eye out if it offends you, cutting off limbs that cause moral offense, putting millstones around your neck, eternal fire, etc. Making allowances for the weight of Redemption and the coming Crucifixion we would have to say that He may have had a few unpleasant things on his mind.

---

[11] Roberts, Paul William, *City in the Desert*, Random House; 1st edition (March 23, 1993)

Nobody enjoys torture and suffering. Jesus, as truly both man and God, likely, has a slightly different human perspective on the whole time and eternity issue now that He has had time to consider things for two thousand years. He moved on, so speak, when He put the Spirit in charge.

There are those who will read this with incredulity—what does he mean that Jesus has had time to consider things for two thousand years—doesn't he know that there is no time in God and that Jesus is one Person subsisting in two natures—human and divine? And to this we can only answer: if Jesus was truly man and truly God, having assumed a human nature, the inability of the man to grow in wisdom, *in time*, would make a mockery of his Humanity. This is, of course, not the traditional Christian position on the matter but it is something to consider. The heresy of Docetism, for example, claimed that the humanity of Jesus was just an illusion.[12] I would suggest that those who have invested the most in the static concept of Jesus as being both perfectly God and perfectly man may have something to gain from further reflection on the matter.[13] A Docetism of personhood is a theological danger that may occur when eternity is used to devalue the meaning of time.

---

[12] A variant of Docetism, for example, might tend to trivialize Jesus' humanity by over-emphasizing the role of his Divinity.

[13] As silly as it may sound, the Second Person of the Trinity cannot take a leave of absence from the Trinity. This suggests either an eternal or a created temporal/aveternal manifestation of the Son, as Jesus Christ. It might be said, of course, that in the perfection of all things within the Trinity, the Incarnation of Jesus is included in an a-priori fashion and only by effect, in time, without any change occurring in God. The question remains: is this entirely true or just a theological assertion?

The notion that God creates *with change occurring in the creature* and not in God[14] becomes problematic when considering the personhood of God. It could be argued that the Incarnation adds nothing to God, in terms of the perfection of His Existence, but it cannot be said that the assumption of a human nature, which occurs in time, adds nothing to humanity, or does not involve a before and after, of some kind, in the perception of the second person of the Trinity relative to His human nature. This can be theologically sloughed off as a mystery or as not adding anything to God that is not already present to God but a further investigation of the relationship between time and eternity is not without merit or the value of increased intelligibility.

Understanding God from multiple perspectives helps us to position ourselves to receive greater truth. From another less controversial and more common sense perspective, for example, we can say that surely God enjoys Himself and that He would like us to do the same—but that there are better ways to do it and there are lesser ways to do it—given that we don't have the big picture. Theologians have often been so focused on what God is not and what God doesn't want us to do that they have missed emphasizing what God is and what it is we, being made in His image and likeness, are to do. The purpose of life cannot be based, simply, on a negative moral assessment of the world or on the notion that we owe something to God other than our love or our allegiance.

---

[14] This is perhaps one of the greatest insights of St. Thomas Aquinas and informs the entirety of his theology.

*By moving from a perspective on God as the great denier, we can see Him for what He really is: the great allower.*[15]

This doesn't mean that everything is allowed but rather that God allows a great deal more than He denies. It is up to us to find the balance between what He allows and what might be unacceptable and that is, indeed, what the pursuit of virtue is all about. Building a political system on this insight may allow us move in the direction of healing the ancient rift between Church and State.

**Bridging the Gap between Church and State**

Current events in Israel, Russia, China and the United States indicate a slide towards a kind of authoritarianism that may be confusing to those who divide the world into good and evil or, simply, liberal and conservative ideologies. The endless, unresolved squabbles between Israelis and Palestinians, the Russian seizure of Crimea, the increasing power of enlightened collectivism in China and the sliding of America away from the authority of the individual towards the authority of the state are all trends that bear further analysis from a different and, perhaps, unique perspective. Issues such as abortion, homosexual marriage and government-run healthcare in the United States are harbingers of a future that the Founding Fathers did not and likely could not imagine.

The future that is unfolding now is coming quickly. The hidden resonance of the unfolding future in the present is, perhaps,

---

[15] This insight comes from the various teachings of Abraham by Bill and Esther Hicks.

greater than our common vocabulary and understanding of history can quickly interpret or summarize. The one thing that is certain is that repeating the mistakes of the past will not guarantee a different outcome nor will the clattering of old rhetoric, without new and creative formulations, stir men's souls.

Nicholas Wolterstorff noted in his 1998 Stone Lectures at Princeton: "In a participatory democracy such as ours, it's important that we each be open with and open to our fellow citizens concerning the deep sources of how we think about political issues" (Lecture 8) This is the first shot across the bow of what Wolterstorff calls "public reason liberalism", which eschews sectarian reasons in political discourse in favor of public ones. Wolterstorff claims that the "dream [of public reason liberalism] has failed" (Lecture 9): present-day disagreements over political issues are as intractable as ever. In that environment, why not give political theology a try in the "space of reasons"? Though political theology is not nearly so popular as in the days of Augustine or Calvin foils–Wolterstorff argues that it's overdue for careful contemporary consideration."[16]

A new kind of authority, it could be argued, is needed in the world; one that recognizes that the only authority worth having comes from both *man and God* with history as a guide for man but not the only guide. Is it possible to re-create an institution

---

[16] *Essays in Political Theology*: http://ndpr.nd.edu/news/45437-the-mighty-and-the-almighty-an-essay-in-political-theology/

that both recognizes divine authority and yet limits the human interpretation of that authority within the calculus and variability of different beliefs and opinions? Can separation of Church and State be less than absolute as it should be but is not in the United States? Would a relative separation, with one influencing the other in the best possible way, be desirable in the world of tomorrow? Is it possible to create a new and better system that mirrors the same kinds of checks and balances that the Founding Fathers created while writing the Declaration of Independence and the Constitution of the United States?

Imagine the world four hundred years from now. What will it look like? Will there be a political role for religion and philosophy in the articulation of solutions for moral and public issues? Will there be a place for human creativity outside of science? Will there be a role for artificial intelligence? What can we do now to manage the future? It is my belief that we are entering the age of a new form of governance that might be called, *The Third Imperium*. This will likely be a fusion of state leadership and corporate free enterprise much as we see operative in China and Russia today. What we do now to build the emerging Imperium, as a moral institution into which the future of the world can adequately unfold, may determine the course of history for centuries to come. First we have to know why we should be concerned.

## Where Does Authority and Creativity Come From?

Rome, as the first empire of the western world, produced a wide range of technical and social innovations. Every time you lift a glass of wine to your lips, for example, remember that it was the Romans who came up with the innovation of storing wine in oak casks instead of clay amphora. Roman cement was also of extraordinary quality. Roman aqueducts and buildings that have remained standing for two thousand years are a testament to its durability. We, likewise, have only to remember that our Senate and House of Representatives are based partly on innovations of the Roman political system.

The Roman Empire might be thought of as the First Imperium; and the Holy Roman Empire, beginning in 800 A.D. under Charlemagne, long after the fall of Rome, ushered in the Second Imperium. The word "imperium," which means roughly, *the power to command,* is emblematic on one hand of all external, political governance and on the other hand, can serve as a metaphor for the internal imperium of the human spirit. The power to command must be reached for from the source of all command and all authority: the energy of life. This power has already been given to us. We all come equipped with it. The power to see it and to use it is conditioned by our conception of ourselves and what we are or are not allowed by society.

The creative person, on the other hand, seems never truly bound by local circumstance, instead they always reach out to what is, to what is possible and to what can be. How this is done almost seems magical or mysterious but it is self-evident that there are those who are more creative than others, in reaching out to transform what might be, into what can be. What is clear is that there is individual creativity, and as seen in Rome, cultural creativity which is produced by individuals working with or employed by institutions.

The American experiment,[17] as it has been called, provides us with many wonderful examples that illustrate the oblique and sometimes puzzling relationship between creativity and personal authority. When we reflect on many of the great men and women of American history, we can only conclude that there are those who seem to resonate with a greater authority than their own.

How did they do this? How did George Washington decide that he had the right to challenge England, the dominant country of his time? Who gave the Wright brothers the authority to fly or which government agency gave them permission? Who told Edison and Tesla to develop new electrical applications? Who told Rockefeller or J.P. Morgan to build their empires? On whose authority did Lucy Stone, Susan B. Anthony or Elizabeth Cady Stanton agitate for a woman's right to vote? Who told Martin Luther King that he had the right to be like everyone else? Who or what inspired Warren Buffett, Bill Gates, Steve Jobs, or Elon Musk in more recent times? What is the relationship between the authority to begin a creative endeavor and its execution? What is the linkage? And more ominously for the future: what sort of authority might an artificial intelligence invoke to express its creativity?

On a more modest note, we might add, who told me to write about authority? How was I enrolled? On whose authority do I write? What or whose "kratos" am I tapping into for this creative endeavor? These are, admittedly, rhetorical questions

---

[17] There are many sources for this idea.
http://www.nccs.net/will-the-great-american-experiment-succeed.php

but they should be considered for the truths that might be harvested. Authority appears to be something that can be tapped into, and like the air we breathe, is so obvious that we tend to gloss over its existence. We sadly only seem to notice it when it is taken away from us or when political circumstances are moving in the direction of its curtailment.

In order to better understand the relationship between authority and creativity, in the present time, we need to return to the cultural, legislative, religious and metaphysical foundation upon which America was built. The flowering of American industry and what has been called "American exceptionalism" [18] cannot be understood without understanding what suppresses creativity. Political institutions that do not support the creativity and initiative of the people do so by un-empowering individuals and vesting authority in the state. The growth of the "permission based" [19] society that America seem to be evolving towards is a direct contradiction to the principles of liberty espoused by the Founding Fathers.

America was founded on *the freedom and authority of the individual as a God-given right* as opposed to institutional rights doled out to human beings by monarchical or other political institutions. This moral dichotomy between the so-called "Divine Right of Kings" and the rights native to a democratic republic is taught by rote in our schools. However, without adverting to the real or divine origin of individual authority, as

---

[18] [WP] http://en.wikipedia.org/wiki/American_exceptionalism
[19] Government Shutdown
http://reason.com/archives/2013/10/15/the-government-shutdown-and-our-permissi

was actually stated in both the Declaration of Independence and the Constitution of the United States, it comes across as a headless abstraction. At the root of this belief in the divine origin of individual authority is an idea that goes back to ancient times, and which was recast eloquently by the Roman lawgiver, Cicero, between 106 and 43 B.C.

**Law Is Not Merely Based on Collective Agreement**

"To Cicero, law was not a matter of written statutes, and lists of regulations, but was a matter deeply ingrained in the human spirit, one that was an integral part of the human experience." In other words, authority was not just external for Cicero but internal. His reasoning was fourfold:

1. *"Humans were created by a higher power or powers (and for the sake of argument, Cicero has the Epicurean Atticus concede the point that this higher power is engaged with the affairs of humanity).*

2. *This higher power which created the universe did, for reasons known to itself, endow humans with a bit of its own divinity, giving the human race the powers of speech, reason, and thought.*

3. *Due to this spark of divinity inside humans, they must de facto be related to the higher power in some fashion.*

4. *Because humans share reason with the higher power, and because this higher power is presumed to be benevolent, it*

*follows that humans, when employing reason correctly, will likewise be benevolent [and share that power]."* [20]

Cicero considers the law to be whatever promotes good and forbids evil. What holds us back from upholding this absolutely is our human failings, our lusts for pleasure, wealth, status [and] other inconsequentials outside of virtue and honor."[21]

Paraphrasing Cicero, we share in the authority and benevolence of this higher power by practicing intellectual and moral excellence or the good habits called virtues. This concept of a dynamic relationship between God and man, *based on likeness,* is at the root of both human authority and political authority for Cicero. Later Christian theological teachings about the children of God are also based on this notion of likeness. Likewise, the infusion of Divine energy in the soul or the Catholic "state of grace" is based on the notion of a conformity of moral and spiritual action with Divine goodness. This understanding of what might be called *a relationship of honor* between God and man is largely absent from modern thinking.

Imagine you love someone. You don't want to do anything that will upset that person or make them think less of you. This is, partly, what I mean about a relationship of honor. We know what will be offensive to the beloved. We must understand then that it is our likeness to God that is the source of our creativity. *The Creator has made all of us creators.* This is a tremendous gift, and in honor of this gift, we need and should

---

[20] [WP]: http://en.wikipedia.org/wiki/De_Legibus
[21] Ibid

want to listen to what He says to us. Honoring this relationship means that if God indicates, either in Scripture or in our hearts, that something is not good, we shouldn't go there. And we know this. Nonetheless, God doesn't force any of us to do anything. He wants us to get it ourselves. He is, perhaps, not quite as hung up on sin as we are, since we frequently use the back and forth of bad behavior as a way to stay away from making lasting spiritual and temporal decisions.

There is, consequently, a kind of odd insult that we level against God when we say "no, you do it—your will be done." What He says back to us in life is: "you do it with me—my will is always present to you." If God wanted to have authority over our lives, He would let us know in short order without resorting to games of peek-a-boo. We know what He wants—that is the law that He has written in our hearts—the law that Cicero celebrates. Everything else is just spiritual gravy.

The Socratic dictum that the purpose of virtue is to make the soul as "good as possible" makes little sense without an understanding of the soul as mirroring, in some way, God's likeness. The ancients simply and rightfully assumed that the soul required additional assistance and support from its original Source. This is, essentially, the basis for the spiritual ecology[22]

---

[22] "The original definition is from Ernst Haeckel, who defined ecology as the study of the relationship of organisms with their environment. In the intervening century and a half, other definitions of ecology have been proposed to reflect growth of the discipline, to found new specialties, or to mark out disciplinary territory." http://www.caryinstitute.org/discover-ecology/definition-ecology

that we commonly call religion, which consists of a series of institutionalized mediations between man and God.

The respective realms of religion and state authority were assumed to have areas of common overlap in the ancient world. There was little need to have the equivalence of separation of church and state in the ancient world. Religious beliefs and politics tended to mirror each other more closely than they do today. What the Gods wanted, the state wanted, and the gods' personal behavior wasn't overly different from that of mankind. The Romans were fairly cosmopolitan about religion. As long as religion didn't interfere with the state, the state wouldn't interfere with religion. And this is also the primary characteristic of an Imperium: the Imperium is a form of governance in which the boundaries of religion and state, or what is called church and state today, are not entirely separate.

This lack of fixed boundaries between religion and state didn't change until Christianity became a fully organized and state sponsored religion, on February 27, 380 A.D, under the co-emperors Gratian and Theodosius the Great. This was done under the edict of Thessalonica. Despite the advantages of having a state religion it should, in reality, be more like having a corporate motto; it should not be entirely exclusive except by popular acclaim. Jump ahead twenty centuries.

## Creativity and Law Are Part of a Larger Ecology

Ecology is, in the broadest sense, the relationship of organisms to their environment.[23] When religion and moral codes form a significant element within a political and social environment, a different kind of ambient ecology is created than might be found in an ecology in which religion and moral codes do not predominate. A moral ecology is the relationship between human beings and their metaphysical, moral, spiritual and even their creative environments. The law, as it is constituted in any culture, is an expression of the beliefs of that culture writ large. When culture is good, the laws tend to reflect that goodness. When the culture is bad the law simply becomes a mirror of that culture's vices.

A good example of what is meant by a moral and spiritual ecology is the teaching of Thomas Aquinas and the medieval scholastics concerning the meaning of evil in relation to various "goods" with a "good" being anything that might be desirable from a non-judgmental or appetitive point of view. Evil was defined as *"the absence of a good that could and should be present."* This indicates that a choice of lesser "goods," than those put forth by conscience, or the soul joined spiritually to the Divine (or some other higher purpose) can lead to negative consequences for the soul and spirit of man.

Any society that considers a legal or spiritual hierarchical relation of "goods" to be chosen, in relation to various "ends"

---

[23] Ibid

or goals must also advert to lesser choices, or what might be called "evils," or those things that take us away from goals. This is, of course, the origin of what we call morality. A society that pretends that there are no objective "goods' to be chosen leaves itself open to the subjective "goods" chosen by appetite. We see the results all around us in the many faces of exploitation. We live in a civilization that has glorified appetitive subjectivity, or what we want, to the exclusion of moral considerations that limit choices based on the possibility of negative moral or spiritual consequences.

The negative effects of bad or poor choices can include psychological disturbances and what is sometimes referred to as *negative emotion*. This is a profound teaching, as it tells us that we must prioritize what we think is good, based on larger standards than our own subjectivity or suffer negative consequences. Consequently, politics might be considered part of a larger ecology of objective meaning rather than simply the legal relations among groups of individuals with differing agendas.

Honor and clear conscience can be thought of as a moral consequence of practicing virtue or good moral and intellectual habits. These good habits, within the ecology of moral and spiritual relations between God and man, help us to be like God. The corollary to this is that an ecology of "viciousness" ultimately develops around those who practice vice or bad habits, and that bad habits have a negative impact on our legal, political and social ecologies. In other words, there are few victimless offenses within a moral and spiritual ecology.

Everyone is affected/effected by what we do and often by what we don't do.

A little imagination regarding the difference between those we consider "clear eyed" and good, or "shifty eyed" and bad, will provide most of us with graphic examples of both virtue and vice. There are people we encounter in everyday life that have "bad vibes" i.e., they resonate with possibly dangerous appetites or what we might call nasty habits. Those who take bad habits to an extreme and who allow themselves to be ruled by a constellation of impulses are usually labeled as criminals or as possessing marginal social skills. How can we understand virtue and vice from a more modern perspective?[24] A list of the intellectual virtues helps us to understand the profound and useful distinction between intellectual and moral virtue.

### The Intellectual Virtues

1. **Science**—in the modern sense of the word, as in technology and the uncovering of cause and effect
2. **Wisdom**—the ability to discern and adequately reflect on inner qualities; to analyze theory or a set of facts in their relation to one another

---

[24] For a larger discussion of the intellectual and moral virtues and the vices as they relate to the landscape of human emotion and psychology see: O'Reilly, Sean, *How to Manage Your Destructive Impulses with Cyber-Kinetics: Redirect Sexual Energy and Discover Your More Enlightened, Spiritually Evolved Self*; published jointly in January 2001 by The Auriga Publishing Group and Ten Speed Press

3. **Understanding**–the intuitive process that allows the mind to directly grasp truth–sometimes without going through all the intellectual steps that might ordinarily be necessary
4. **Prudence**–The ability to govern and control oneself through reason
5. **Art**–understood in the sense of artistic craftsmanship, as in sculpture, painting, music or a life well-lived

The discipline of psychology provides a unique schematic to model the energy preserved by virtue and show how energy is consumed by vice. The opposition to the instinctual energies of the Id[25] in Freudian psychology, in order to sublimate and convert the energy of impulse into civilized action, is well-documented; it is also well-attested to by anecdotal and personal experience. We know that we cannot allow every stray impulse to take root in our lives. The problem is that most people don't have a moral or a metaphysical map to guide them through the maze of their personal impulses. As James Davidson noted in his book, *Courtesans and Fishcakes*:

*"In classical Athens, whether the struggle was between you and the world's pleasures, or between you and your body, this state of conflict was normal and natural. What was abnormal was to put up no resistance, to be continually and instantly overwhelmed. Such feeble characters threw in the towel without a fight. They were defeated and enslaved by their desires. They were known as the akolastoi, the uncorrected, the unchecked, the unbridled, or the akrateis, the powerless, the impotent, the incontinent."*

---

[25] Freud, Sigmund, *The Ego and the Id*, W.W. Norton and Company, Copyright 1960, page 14

Can you imagine a politician talking about this today? The metaphysical relationship of sexual energy to the ecosystem of human consciousness and the social order is illustrated in the ground-breaking book, *How to Manage Your Destructive Impulses with Cyber-Kinetics*[26] published in 2001. Understanding how the energy and movement of the soul relates to choices that improve the power of creativity is critical to understanding the notions of social evolution through virtue and social devolution via vice.

The derivation of power and conversion to creative energy is often linked (although not exclusively) to a sublimation of appetitive power or what Freud referred to as the instinctual energy of the Id. Freud called this conversion of appetitive energy into more productive channels *sublimation*[27] and the way this energy is creatively invested in activities, objects and ideas (including ideals) is referred to as *cathection*. The ancients would have referred to this as virtue, i.e., that excellence has to be something that is invested in activity by choice. Vice is the absence of this kind of choosing and results in a psychological return to the default position of pure appetite. Appetite is simply what you want, whenever you want it.

What happens when this sublimated energy or virtue "cathects" with spirituality may be the locus of all creativity. We have only

---

[26] O'Reilly, Sean, *How to Manage Your Destructive Impulses with Cyber-Kinetics: Redirect Sexual Energy and Discover Your More Enlightened, Spiritually Evolved Self*; published jointly in January 2001 by The Auriga Publishing Group and Ten Speed Press

[27] Freud, Sigmund, *The Ego and the Id*. W. W Norton and Company, Copyright 1960, page 35

to think about the celibate Irish monks who brought Christianity to Europe to realize the power that sublimated energy can have when it meets the power of divine intentionality.[28]

Ayn Rand, in the *Anatomy of Compromise*, noted the opposite effect of what happens when the virtue of sublimation is not engaged, when impulses are favored and the cathection so necessary for creativity languishes:

*"A major symptom of a man's or a culture's intellectual and moral disintegration is the shrinking of vision and goals to the concrete-bound range of the immediate moment. This means: The progressive disappearance of abstractions from a man's mental processes or from a society's concerns. The manifestation of a disintegrating consciousness is the inability to think and act in terms of principles."*

The aspersions cast upon those who seem unable to interrogate or check their appetites is a common source of amusement. The extremely obese, the greedy and the cheap, the overly talkative, the cruel, the dishonest, and those driven by an extreme need to "get off" under all circumstances are frequently the butt of jokes around the office cooler. Those with excessive appetites are seldom looked up to as model citizens. A list of the moral virtues shows us how the moral virtues are distinguished from the intellectual virtues.

The moral virtues are excellences of the will, while the intellectual virtues are excellences of mind. This is why some highly intelligent people can be moral imbeciles and why those

---

[28] We might say that when cathection is understood from the perspective of joint creative action between man and God that it is a forge of almost infinite power.

individuals with excellent morals can have better character than those who may have more natural intelligence. Virtue might be thought of as a tool for improving our relationship with both ourselves and others.

## The Moral Virtues

1. **Courage**–the power to face adversity and struggle against evils
2. **Continence**–self-restraint in reference to your appetites or desires
3. **Liberality**–generous giving which overcomes greed
4. **Magnificence**–the ability to spend money on large, possibly useful and usually beautiful projects
5. **Magnanimity**–the magnanimous person is able to overlook slights and insults, and rise above pettiness. He or she is generous and able to get work done without complaint.
6. **Honor**–a state of character which is a result of the practice of moral and intellectual excellence
7. **Gentleness**–to deal with others on the basis of kindness and compassion
8. **Friendship**–friendship outside of casual acquaintances, requires effort to cultivate
9. **Temperance**–self-restraint in regards to pleasure
10. **Truthfulness**–the ability to see and affirm what is, and deny what is not
11. **Justice**–seeking for others and yourself that to which all are entitled under both moral and social law

The vices opposed to the virtues then become self-evident, as in, lying can be considered the vice opposed to the moral virtue of truthfulness, or niggardliness can be thought of as the vice opposed to the moral virtue of magnificence. The negative characterization of masturbation, for example, as a kind of "pollution,"[29] or form of incontinence, lasting up to about the middle of the 20th century marks the boundary line between the Christian notion of sexuality, as being on a continuum of honor between God and man, and the more modern conception of sexuality as simply a toilet function. The older notion of masturbation, as an intellectually unregulated, agent of disordered appetite is now openly mocked. Sexuality, stripped from any relationship with God, is open to whatever interpretation society, guided by the moral Frankenstein of positivism,[30] gives it. Sexuality without commitment and spirituality tends to be untethered. Where is honor and courage as it might relate to sexuality today? Honor and courage are required as much, if not more, in the realm of sexuality as in any other area of moral endeavor. It is a national disgrace that sexuality has been relegated to that of a toilet function by many politicians, judges and social scientists.

---

[29] Mostly Family:
http://www.mostholyfamilymonastery.com/masturbation_a_sin.php

[30] As a philosophical system or method, Positivism denies the validity of metaphysical speculations, and maintains that the data of sense experience are the only object and the supreme criterion of human knowledge. In law it means that the law is self-referential with no outside or objective natural law to influence it.

Creativity makes little sense unless the energy behind creativity can be accounted for. Whether this is described as the instinctual energies of the Id, Psychic Energy, Chi or Kundalini,[31] a model is needed to show the relationship of energy-dissipating activities that may limit creativity, and energy-conserving activities that may enhance creativity. The ancient model of virtue and vice makes more sense when it is related to a gauge or a model of energy consumption. The notion of a natural life-energy or force that requires replenishment provides a useful illustration for the activities of moral excess that waste energy. Furthermore, understanding how life energy might be related to the energies of the Divine, provides a tapestry upon which the story of grace might be told.

## Natural Law and Virtue Also Apply to the State

Returning to Cicero as a corrective against all those who assert that the law is "positive"[32] or that cause and effect are an illusion, we can say that without cause and effect, or the notion of creation, no form of morality, subjective or objective, can be asserted as being superior to another. "Not only right and wrong are [causally] distinguished by nature," writes Cicero, "but also in general all honorable and disgraceful things. For nature makes common understandings for us and starts forming

---

[31] This ecology is articulated in *How to Manage Your Destructive Impulses with Cyber-Kinetics*; Sean O'Reilly, Ten Speed Press, January 2001

[32] Positivism denies the validity of metaphysical speculations, and maintains that the data of sense experience are the only object and the supreme criterion of human knowledge. In law it means that the law is self-referential with no outside or objective natural law to influence it.

them in our minds so that honorable things are based on virtue, disgraceful things on vices" (1.44). In Book One of *On Duties*, there is an explanation of the basic human inclinations that give rise, with reason's guidance, to the foundational (later to be called "cardinal") virtues of wisdom, justice, courage and temperance/moderation. Finding these virtues is the way to discover nature's [plan for humanity], to [understanding] the law of nature and thereby what is right."[33] In other words, there is an algorithm, a methodology for discovering good behavior that is written in the heart of human nature.

"Cicero transmitted the Greek Stoic idea of a moral higher law to the modern world. In his dialogue De Legibus (On the Laws, 52 B.C.), he talked about the supreme law which existed through the ages, before the mention of any written law or established state. He also referred to it as the law of nature for the source of right.[34] In *De Republica* (The Republic, 51 B.C.) he says:

*"True law is right reason in agreement with nature; it is of universal application, unchanging and everlasting. . .there will not be different laws at Rome and at Athens, or different laws now and in the future, but one eternal and unchangeable law will be valid for all nations and all times, and there will be one master and ruler, God, over us all, for he is the author of this law, its promulgator, and its enforcing judge. Whoever is disobedient is fleeing from himself and denying his human nature, and by reason of this very fact he will suffer the worst*

---

[33] http://www.nlnrac.org/classical/cicero
[34] Cicero: http://www.nlnrac.org/classical/cicero

*penalties even if he escapes what is commonly considered punishment."* [35]

Forgive me for lingering over the contributions of Cicero to common sense but has anyone ever stated the relationship between the authority of God and society more forcefully? Cicero's explanation of what later became known as Natural Law, as mediating between the authority of God and man, is timeless. Bearing in mind that Cicero lived before the founding of Christianity, universal moral concepts from the Greeks and the Romans that antedate Christianity are useful in the modern world, which is rapidly approaching a post-Christian state. Natural law[36] has been cast aside by those brandishing a new creed: that of a universe without causality and without moral laws. This is the world of atheistic science and political positivism[37] where nothing really exists except for what is in your head or on paper. It is this subjective world view that cannot accept any authority, which is not granted by the state,

---

[35] Ibid

[36] Think of Natural Law as a kind of Divine or spiritual, cloud-based moral architecture. Using the cloud, as a metaphor from computer programming and system architecture, we can say that we all have access to this cloud-based system of values via the operating system of our souls.

[37] Positivism is a system of philosophical and religious doctrines elaborated by Auguste Comte. As a philosophical system or method, Positivism denies the validity of metaphysical speculations, and maintains that the data of sense experience are the only object and the supreme criterion of human knowledge; as a religious system, it denies the existence of a personal God and takes humanity, "the great being", as the object of its veneration and cult

as it recognizes only the legal authority of political institutions and not the objective moral and spiritual authority of a higher entity—since those things are assumed not to exist.

*"While Cicero derived many ideas from the Greeks, he also contributed some key ideas of his own. Greek philosophers had conceived of society and government as virtually the same, coming together in the polis (city-state).* **Cicero declared that government is like a trustee, morally obliged to serve society**—*which means society is something larger and separate. Appreciation for the myriad wonders of civil society, where private individuals develop languages, markets, legal customs, and other institutions, didn't come until the eighteenth century, but it was Cicero who began to see the light."* [38]

"Cicero was the first to say that government was justified primarily as a means of protecting private property. Both Plato and Aristotle had imagined that government could be used to improve morals. [In this sense, government can and should contribute to the process of moral self-improvement by adhering to Natural Law.] Neither Plato nor Aristotle, however, had conceived of private property—an absolute claim to something over everyone else [as one of the primary functions of government]."[39]

Cicero's *De Officiis* (*On Duties*, 44 B.C.) notes: "The chief purpose in the establishment of states and constitutional orders was that individual property rights might be secured . . . it is the peculiar function of state and city to guarantee to every man

---

[38] Cicero: http://www.fee.org/the_freeman/detail/marcus-tullius-cicero-who-gave-natural-law-to-the-modern-world
[39] Ibid

the free and undisturbed control of his own property. Again: The men who administer public affairs must first of all see that everyone holds onto what is his, and that private men are never deprived of their goods by public men." [40]

The Founding Fathers of America, who were highly conversant with Greek and Roman moral philosophy, never intended the separation of Church and State to become a separation of morality and the state, or a rigid separation between atheistic morality and Christian morality as the trend is today. It should be clear to everyone that murder, theft, rape, sodomy[41] and abortion, for example, are not just sins against a religious code but are offenses against a common moral code.

## The Meaning of Imperium Is Currently Divided by Church and State

As we see the world sliding towards various kinds of authoritarianism, often even masquerading as democracy, it is enlightening to reflect again on the meaning of authority as understood by the Roman Empire of Cicero's time. The Latin word "imperium" roughly means *the power to command* and was distinguished from the other related word *regnum*, which referred only to royal power. Imperium was, essentially, military command. Our English word emperor, for example, is derived from the word. Imperium also referred, in a general sense, to

---

[40] Ibid

[41] Specifically, and in this instance, anal sex between consenting adults of either sex

the power of the state over the individual. Imperium, as previously stated, in the larger sense means the power of authority to command[42] and it is this meaning that can be applied to the development of a new Imperium for the present age.

Imperium also means the ruling authority of the Catholic Church, which is distinguished from the Magisterium or the teaching authority of the Church. (Imperium is a term that is little used at the present time as it more properly belongs to civil governance.) Authority must be held and regulated somewhere in society or within a religious or military group or it will default to being held by those who are the strongest and the most ruthless. We are so accustomed to democracy that we find it hard to imagine that rule, where power is held by a republican form of governance, imbued with spiritual and moral principles, may be preferable to the rule of the mob. A democracy is only as good as the people who constitute such a system and without virtue, the vices of the public will be mirrored in the laws of the Republic.[43]

---

[42] Hugh Chisholm, *The Encyclopædia Britannica*: a dictionary of arts, sciences ..., Volume 9, pg. 348, 1910

[43] A republic is a form of government in which power resides in the people, and the government is ruled by elected leaders run according to law (from Latin: res publica), rather than inherited or appointed (such as through inheritance or divine mandate). In modern times the definition of a republic is also commonly limited to a government which excludes a monarch. Currently, 135 of the world's 206 sovereign states use the word "republic" as part of their official names. [WP]

The Imperium of the Holy Roman Empire, which succeeded the western empire after the fall of Rome was a watershed event. "In 410 A.D., the Visigoths, [a Germanic tribe] led by Alaric, breached the walls of Rome and sacked the capital of the Roman Empire. The Visigoths looted, burned, and pillaged their way through the city, leaving a wake of destruction wherever they went. The plundering continued for three days. For the first time in nearly a millennium, the city of Rome was in the hands of someone other than the Romans. This was the first time that the city of Rome was sacked, but by no means the last." In 476 A.D. Romulus, the last of the Roman emperors in the west, was overthrown by the Germanic leader Odoacer, who became the first Barbarian to rule in Rome. The order that the Roman Empire had brought to Western Europe for 1,000 years was no more." [44]

Following the fall of Rome, a series of events set into motion by many holy men and women, took place on Christmas in three different eras that set the stage for the Second Imperium.

1. The conversion of Clovis, Frankish King of Gaul, in 595 A.D.
2. The final conversion of England to Christianity in 680 A.D
3. The crowning of Charlemagne (also a Germanic Frank)[45] as head of the Holy Roman Empire in 800 A.D.

*"Three hundred years after [St. Augustine of Canterbury's mass baptisms at York], God gives us another glorious event in honor of the Birth-Day of his Son. It was on this divine Anniversary, in the year 800,*

---

[44] http://www.ushistory.org/civ/6f.asp
[45] The Franks, were a Germanic tribe in present-day Belgium, France, Luxembourg, the Netherlands and western Germany.

*and at Rome, in the Basilica of St. Peter, that was created the Holy Roman Empire, to which God assigned the grand mission of propagating the Kingdom of Christ among the barbarian nations of the North, and of upholding, under the direction of the Sovereign Pontiffs, the confederation and unity of Europe. St. Leo III crowned Charlemagne Emperor. Here, then, was a new Caesar, a new Augustus, on the earth; not, indeed, a successor of those ancient Lords of Pagan Rome, but one who was invested with the title and power by the Vicar of Him, who is called, in the Sacred Scriptures, King of Kings, and Lord of Lords."* [46]

The Holy Roman Empire, in Constantinople (now modern day Istanbul), inherited the mantle of Rome and this was the beginning of a very long dance between the Church and civil authority. The Church assumed an authority that transcended civil authority much in the same way that Islam fuses religion and state today in a theocracy. Given that religious and civil authority are two very different orders, embracing two different worlds, it is usually impossible for one to stop interfering in the affairs of the other without a clear demarcation and understanding of what it is that each is to govern. Human authority and divine authority are two different realms and require *relative separation* in order for each to keep an appropriate distance from the other. Like electrons in "shells" around the atom, the distance, not the closeness, between church and state is what has made the relationship functional in the modern world.

---

[46] http://catholicism.org/sacrum-imperium.html

Pope Gregory the Ninth used the term "Imperium Animarum" or power over souls to buttress his authority in continuing arguments with the Holy Roman Emperor Frederick II (1194-1250 A.D.) who wanted the empire to have civic authority over the church.[47] The German Frederick, who was born in Italy, referred to himself as King of the Romans and consequently [at least in his mind] King of Jerusalem. Frederick established a modern bureaucracy. His empire extended from Sicily through Italy and included much of present day Germany. He was, apparently, an enormously gifted and energetic man who exercised authority along the lines of Aristotle's virtue of magnificence. His own sense of authority, however, was often at odds with the institutional authority of the Popes.

This conflict between civil and religious authority had additional roots in what was called, the *imperium in imperio* which referred to the state within a state, presumably the Imperium of religious authority over or within the state. Henry the XIII of England objected to this kind of power, exercised by the Church of Rome, as late as 1533. The English parliamentary action, *Act of Restraint of Appeals,* attempted to do away with the power of the Catholic Church and vest it solely in the English crown.[48] This is also part of the modern origin of the centuries-old squabble between church and state.

The conclusion that can be drawn from the conflict between Church and State is that the conception of necessary social rules in order to keep people from falling off the spiritual map can be

---

[47] [WP]: http://en.wikipedia.org/wiki/De_Legibus
[48] Ibid

overdone—way overdone. It can be further concluded that the authority of Church and state should be considered as an original and necessary unity, or as two sides of the same coin, and not as separate entities in conflict. Didn't Jesus say, "Render unto Caesar what is Caesar's and render unto God what is God's"? The time has come to end the old, counterproductive division between Church and State and create a new synthesis that will take advantage of the strengths of both. God perceived as a "denier" leads to a completely different take on authority than does asserting that God is an "allower". We've gone down the road of God as the great denier and it doesn't work.

## The Holy Roman Empire and Empire Building Today

The Holy Roman Empire actually continued on as late as the early 19th century, although by that time it had degenerated into a caricature of its former self. One can imagine nobles shuffling titles like decks of cards and vying for the attention of various courts based on those titles but having long forgotten that empire must have force and purpose behind it to mean anything.

*"At this time it was centralized in the loosely defined and allied Germanic states/kingdoms. Following the rise of Napoleon and the defeat of many different, unaligned German kingdoms' forces by Napoleon's forces, Napoleon was able to sweep across the nation we now know as Germany. One of the first things Napoleon did was to dismantle the once-proud Holy Roman Empire as well as install a number of administrative and economic reforms. Doing so actually laid the foundations of a (loose) sense of German nationalism that had not existed prior to this and led the way to many of the revolutionary happenings of the 19th century in central Europe (more specifically in*

*Germany, Prussia, Hungary, Austria, Denmark, France, and many other tiny German principalities and duchies)."* [49]

It is interesting to note, in retrospect, that not only did the Germanic peoples ultimately conquer Rome, they were among the continuing and last remnants of the Holy Roman Empire before it was swept away by Napoleon. The echoes of empire and the disenfranchisement of the German people in regards to the former borders of Germanic Austria were keenly felt by Adolph Hitler and played a role in his establishment of the Third Reich.[50]

"Napoleon [once] sarcastically remarked that Germany was always 'becoming, not being', but in the long run, ironically enough, the consequence of his policies would be the stimulation of German nationalism and the emergence of a united Germany which would humble the French in the two World Wars."[51] The echoes and consequences of empire still reverberate in Europe in a way that is hard for the average American to grasp. What is happening financially and economically in Europe and the rest of the world is, however, resonant with the old patterns of conquest.

As recently as 2011, British journalist Simon Heffer wrote, "Where Hitler failed by military means to conquer Europe, modern Germans are succeeding through trade and financial

---

[49]http://history.stackexchange.com/questions/13/when-did-the-holy-roman-empire-collapse
[50] *Mein Kampf*
[51] http://www.historytoday.com/richard-cavendish/end-holy-roman-empire

discipline. Welcome to the Fourth Reich."[52] The same has also been said of the Japanese in their island purchases throughout the former south pacific war theater. Even Hawaii is emerging as a Japanese economic colony. These trends are visible in other ways, too.

According to Andrey Fursov, Historian of the Institute of Scientific Information on Social Sciences of the Russian Academy of Sciences: "147 companies, 1% of all companies, controlled 40% of the world economy. This is very indicative. This means that the modern economy, whose basic unit of analysis is the market, conceals more than it shows. Politics and the nation-state are fading away, and this means that political science, with its basic units of analysis—politics and the state—not only cannot adequately conceptualize, but cannot even merely depict real power relations, especially on the global level."[53] The creation and expansion of political institutions that are fueled by economic acquisition and development is the emerging trend upon which the notion of the Third Imperium is based.

The word "Imperium," with its long and suggestive history, can be applied to the present moral circumstances of today's world as a way of beginning to recast the way we think and act politically, by observing the mistakes of the past and using those mistakes to create a new and more cordial relationship between church and state, and forge economic enterprises of benefit to the world at large. The emergence of radical Islam makes this a

---

[52] http://en.wikipedia.org/wiki/Fourth_Reich
[53] http://newparadigm.schillerinstitute.com/media/andrey-fursov-the-current-world-crisis-its-social-nature-and-challenge-to-social-science/

more urgent task than ever before, as the cultural unity created by a union of religion and state has a great deal of emotional power. Whatever form or name the Third Imperium takes, the outlines of its emergence can be seen in the rise of Islam and the vast conglomerates of economic and political power that constitute the amorphous and authoritarian regimes in Russia and China today. The real question that is before the West concerns what kind of belief system the future governance of the world will be driven by. Will it be driven by atheism or an open house of religious, moral and secular beliefs?

# II

# Causality Connects Everything

"Can you also, Lucullus, affirm that there is any power united with wisdom and prudence which has made, or, to use your own expression, manufactured man? What sort of a manufacture is that? Where is it exercised? When? Why? How?"

-Cicero, *Academica*, Book II, Chapter XXVII, section 87

## Covenants between God and Man

The Bible speaks about covenants between man and God, which reaffirms the linkage between time and eternity. The Old Testament is part of the old covenant and the New Testament is part of the new covenant between man and God brokered by Jesus Christ. This is a way of dividing history into a kind of before and after Christ. This is, of course, the origin of B.C. (before Christ) and A.D. (Anno Domini or in the year of our Lord)[54]. However true this division of history may be it is not enough. God's testament to us is not limited by the past or simply to the written word. We must consider that God is continually revealing Himself. This is the eternal covenant. "The Father desires," as Jesus says, "worshippers in Spirit and Truth." This means that we are not to be slaves to what was but to what "is" and what should be. The ultimate authority and source of "ought" is the Holy Trinity,[55] which, in metaphysical terms, "Is" its own existence. The ultimate authority of the Third Imperium, if it is to have any force at all outside of earthly power, is in the desire of the Father to have the earthly Kingdom mirror the heavenly Kingdom.

God's authority, while it may be considered in the abstract as absolute is, and from the point of view of those of us in time,

---

[54] Note that the politically correct in academia, who developed the politically correct notion of B.C.E. (Before the Common Era) and C.E. (the Common Era), miss the boat completely. There was nothing common about, or even now commonly held, about the era that developed after the birth of Christ.

[55] The Father as God Being Himself, the Son as God knowing Himself, the Spirit as God loving Himself (formulation by Tim O'Reilly)

*other than, but not unlike* our own authority. If our authority is based on our likeness to God, then His power is our power through the magic of participation. Faith is the ultimate merger of our power with that of the Divine. It is a sublimation of our will and appetites to a greater will and an effortless kratos that literally has no limits. This is why Jesus was insistent that:

*"If you had faith you could say to the mountain throw yourself into the sea and it would be done."*

What God, having given such authority to His children, would have any need to contradict that authority? It should be clear for even the most casual observer that God allows just about anything to take place in His world without interference. The consequences, for good or ill, of God's tolerance are all around us. This kind of tolerance should be used in crafting the political structures of the Third Imperium. Ultimately all virtue, all goodness must be by choice and not coercion.

If we think about God and our likeness to God[56] as the manifest source of authority and creativity for individuals, then the earthly and political manifestation of that relationship should reflect the wisdom of the Celestial Kingdom. One should guarantee and support the other. Beyond this, however, in radiant splendor is the truth that the Kingdom of God on earth will be something new and not merely a reditus[57] of merit. If God simply wanted a return of the all to the All, it would have to be concluded that this is a very bad set-up. Clearly this is not the

---

[56] Here assume the Christian God; the Holy Trinity of Father, Son and Holy Spirit.
[57] The return of the all to the All; also elucidated by Maximus the Confessor.

case. God made lesser creators in humanity, and in this, even the angels may be jealous as they cannot change their minds the way we do.[58] God's covenant with mankind is that he made us creators and not slaves on some sort of assembly line to heaven. God wants us to "get it"—not just to get to it.

## Gnosticism and the Artifacts of Eternity

If we consider elements of the Old and New Testament as a metaphor for something not fully understood, we might say that what the Trinity is doing in the creation, from start to finish, is establishing the heavenly kingdom, including Father, Son and Holy Spirit, in an entirely new order of participated being. This is not for God's benefit but for our benefit. Creation, in this respect, is roughly analogous to what we might describe as a virtual, evolving reality. The entire order of participated and contingent being, including time, might be thought of, simply, as an artifact of eternity. All of creation, as we know it, occurs within this artifact, or secondary level of created being, existing contingently just outside the Divine Essence.

*This means that there are only two things in the universe: what is created and what is uncreated. The notion of what is created may be in need of some extension.*

Some have referred to this notion as, *aveternity,* or a kind of secondary eternity that had a beginning but no end. Others, like the Greek Orthodox monk, Gregory Palamas (1296-1359 A.D.) referred to a distinction between the divine essence and the

---

[58] The theory is that angels' decisions are irrevocable given the close fusion of their essences with their existence.

"divine energies."[59] The teaching on the divine energies is well established in Eastern Orthodox theology and has a long tradition going back more than 2,000 years, likely originating in the mystical teachings of Plato and later, in the works of Plotinus.[60]

*"The divine energies might be described as that mode of existence of the Trinity which is outside of its inaccessible essence. God thus exists in His essence and outside of His essence."* [61]

However described, the artifacts of eternity or everything that is created, are based on the common assumption and conclusion that there can be no before and after in God, therefore any consideration of quasi-temporal events involving God, such as the Incarnation or the Light on Mount Tabor, during the Transfiguration, or even relations between the Persons of the Trinity must be re-considered from within a metaphysical construct that allows the mediation of time. This is similar to Plotinus's doctrine on the One[62] with everything that is not the One being an "emanation" or a secondary order of existence from that of the One, which is identified as God.

---

[59] G. Palamas: http://orthodoxinfo.com/phronema/florov_palamas.aspx
[60] http://en.wikipedia.org/wiki/Plotinus
[61] Lossky, as quoted in A. N. Williams, *The Ground of Union: Deification in Aquinas and Palamas*, Oxford University Press, 1999, page 140

[62] The One is not just an intellectual conception but something that can be experienced, an experience where one goes beyond all multiplicity. Plotinus writes, "We ought not even to say that he will *see*, but he will *be* that which he sees, if indeed it is possible any longer to distinguish between seer and seen, and not boldly to affirm that the two are one." http://en.wikipedia.org/wiki/Plotinus

Plotinus was a Neo-Platonist of the first century AD who reworked Plato's notion of the *Demiurge,* a subordinate deity, who fashions the sensible world in the light of eternal ideas into a more coherent set of teachings. "According to Valentinian[63] tradition, the Demiurge is formed as an "an image of the Father" (Excepts of Theodotus 47:1-3). A similar description occurs in the Tripartite Tractate: "He is the lord of all of them, that is, the countenance which the logos (i.e., Sophia) brought forth in his thought as a representation of the Father of the Totalities. Therefore, he is adorned with every name which is a representation of him, since he is characterized by every property and glorious quality. For he too is called 'father' and 'god' and 'demiurge' and 'king' and 'judge' and 'place' and 'dwelling' and 'law'. Because he is seen as the image of the true God and Father, Valentinians have no problem using the terms "Father" and "God" to describe him (cf. also *Against Heresies* 1:5:1, Valentinian Exposition 38). While he is an image of the true God, he is not a perfect on account of his non-spiritual nature. In comparison with the true God he is rather "coarse" or "rough" (Excerpts of Theodotus 33:4)."[64]

The Christian teaching on the Trinity, which appears at first glance, to be radically different than either Plato's or Plotinus's theory of emanation has, perhaps, more in common with these

---

[63] Gnostic Society Library: "Valentinus was one of the most influential Gnostic Christian teachers of the second century A.D. He founded a movement which spread throughout Europe, the Middle East and North Africa. Despite persecution by the Catholic Church, the Valentinian School endured for over 600 years."

[64] http://www.gnosis.org/library/valentinus/Demiurge.htm

ideas than not. The Three Persons of the Trinity are one and yet the One is actually Three. This is a paradox that can be restated as two questions. If the Three Persons are fundamentally one, how are they One, and how are they simultaneously also Three? Using the teaching of the divine energies, we might think of the persons of God as follows: *One as God exists in His Essence and Three as He exists outside His essence*. The two modes are equivalent in that the One is what is predicated from the perspective of eternity and Existence, and the Triune is what is glimpsed from the perspective of essence and time.

The traditional teaching in this regard is that the paradox consists of the One also being fundamentally Three, not One and then Three but this presupposes an opposition of time and eternity in God. We are, perhaps, looking at it the problem with the wrong filters.

*When the Father regards Himself, (as He does eternally) He also sees Himself in all the possible ways that He might be seen and understood. He is also eternally understood and loved by the Son and the Holy Spirit as He loves Them. This loving and understanding occurs without movement both in eternity and time. Imagine that thousands of races across the universe have seen the Three faces of God and that God has always seen through all eyes—ours and theirs—yesterday, today and for all the tomorrows to ever be.*

The division of everything that exists into what is Uncreated and Created may reiterate this dual modality of Existence. Existence doesn't exist[65] in the traditional sense of the word because it

---

[65] Wilhelmson, Frederick, *The Paradoxical Structure of Existence,* The University of Dallas Press, 1970

doesn't come forth from anything other than Itself and yet it does exist precisely because its existence is self-caused—in and through Itself. (We call it existence but what it is in itself is entirely different from anything that we are used to in our current perception or experience.) When creation occurs, it must occur in time because creation presumes a before and after. Creation involves a kind of immediate downshifting to essence in time and then a long, slow up-shifting back to Existence and Eternity via evolution and redemption. Time is the clutch in the machinery of eternity as the All returns to its Source.

This, admittedly, Gnostic notion of the all returning to the All is an idea that extends from the time of Plato, through Plotinus and the early church Fathers, all the way to Meister Eckhart and to metaphysicians of the present day. One of the most important Christian proponents was John Scottus Eriugena, a ninth century Irishman.[66] He essentially reworked the Neo-Platonic tradition and put it into the service of Christianity. His

---

[66] "Johannes (800 AD–877 AD), who signed himself as 'Eriugena' in one manuscript, and who was referred to by his contemporaries as 'the Irishman' (*scottus* — in the 9th century Ireland was referred to as '*Scotia Maior*' and its inhabitants as '*scotti*') is the most significant Irish intellectual of the early monastic period. He is generally recognized to be both the outstanding philosopher (in terms of originality) of the Carolingian era and of the whole period of Latin philosophy stretching from Boethius to Anselm. Eriugena is also, though this parallel remains to be explored, more or less a contemporary of the Arab Neo-Platonist Al-Kindi. Since the seventeenth century, it has become usual to refer to this Irish philosopher as John Scottus (or 'Scotus') Eriugena to distinguish him from the thirteenth-century John Duns Scotus...Eriugena's uniqueness lies in the fact that, quite remarkably for a scholar in Western Europe in the Carolingian era, he had considerable familiarity with the Greek language, affording him access to the Greek Christian theological tradition, from the Cappadocians to Gregory of Nyssa, hitherto almost entirely unknown in the Latin West. http://plato.stanford.edu/entries/scottus-eriugena/

thinking is neither well-subscribed to nor well-understood today but he may well have been, along with Aquinas and the later Duns Scotus, one of the three greatest minds of the medieval period.

"Eriugena's thought is best understood as a sustained attempt to create a consistent, systematic, Christian Neoplatonism from diverse but primarily Christian sources. Eriugena had a unique gift for identifying the underlying intellectual framework, broadly Neo-platonic but also deeply Christian, assumed by the writers of the Christian East... Overall, Eriugena develops a Neo-platonic cosmology according to which the infinite, transcendent and 'unknown' God, who is beyond being and non-being, through a process of self-articulation, procession, or 'self-creation', proceeds from his divine 'darkness' or 'non-being' into the light of being, speaking the Word who is understood as Christ, and at the same timeless moment bringing forth the primary causes of all creation. These causes in turn proceed into their created effects and as such are creatures entirely dependent on, and will ultimately return to their sources, which are the Causes or Ideas in God. These Causes, considered as diverse and infinite in themselves, are actually one single principle in the divine One."[67]

Using the perspective of a Christianized Gnosticism, we can say that there is no effort on God's part to shift gears and create, and creation occurs out of nothing—no-thing with time being the necessary and first result of creation. The before and after is in relation to the thing created, not in the Creator but in the

---

[67] http://plato.stanford.edu/entries/scottus-eriugena/

contingent existence of the thing created that has been known from eternity. If it is true that time and everything in it has been known from eternity, then this knowledge is not, however, quite the same thing as nothing. It is, in the words of another Scot, Dun Scotus, an *ens diminutum*, a little being. The notion of a "little being" points to the potential paradox of eternal time. If it is true that the matter and energy of the universe has always existed, then it may be that God's binary mode of existence will help bridge the gap between atheism and religion. The argument is really between whether or not God is personal or impersonal. God as both One and Three enables a bridging of both arguments and could act as a unifying principle for opposing religious ideologies.

## Why God's Existence in Time is Important

There is a suspicion among western academics that the intolerance of organized religion is such that religion and science can have no part of each other. This is based on a false premise, viz., that the God of religion is an absolute God so removed from human affairs that obedience or damnation are the only two possible venues for human activity. This assumption of limitation, in terms of spiritual choice is, unfortunately, an accurate description of religious fundamentalism. The past intolerances of the Roman Catholic Church (of which I am a member) and the radical intolerances of Islam come to mind. This is the God who says: "my way or the highway." The millions of followers of some sects who believe that only one understanding of God is acceptable has led to an extraordinary amount of violence in God's name. The absurdity of killing in the name of God by both Christians and Moslems is such a departure from the obvious path of divinity as to be nearly satanic. The importance of a God whose divine energies exist outside of the Divine Essence might be described as a vast causal metaphor for spiritual understanding and allowance.

A God who was and is able to walk among us is surely worth paying attention to and far more than any prophet, seer or politician who might claim otherwise. A God so remote from human affairs that He requires mindless obedience to a set of precepts or laws is a projection of human fear and inadequacy. Indeed, it might be argued that it was for this reason that Jesus came into the world: to save us from false Gods and Gods who don't deliver the goods.

Jesus never wrote anything down, other than in sand, when he, likely, wrote down the sins of those who were preparing to stone a woman accused of adultery. The message is clear: what is written is not as important as what is morally and spiritually self-evident.[68] This also applies, to some extent, to what we see in scripture. What is written down, despite any assurances of divinely guaranteed accuracy, is still what might be called hearsay. If it resonates believe it; if it does not resonate, take it with a grain of salt. Truth has a power beyond words and dithering over fine shades of meaning is often an excuse for delaying right action.

---

[68] "Legalism is one of the most insidious, and deadliest, dangers which Christians face. It is insidious because it is a constant temptation which arises from the depths of our old, fleshly nature—hence it is a familiar, even comfortable urge. http://www.disciplemagazine.com/www/articles/166.740

God has identified Himself so closely with matter that He assumed a human nature. This act injects, so to speak, the freedom of heaven into earthly existence. This represents a transmogrification or elevation and change of the entire material order into something more than matter governed by only physical rules. God's freedom is absolute and this radical character of God's freedom is celebrated by all free men and women as their birthright. We have freedom because God is freedom. The primary lesson of the New Testament is that God does not desire sacrifice but free obedience to the Three Persons of the one God, which can only be mediated and understood by a heart possessed of love and a mind annealed to goodness. Does anyone possessing an ounce of rationality think that God cares for anything other than a pure heart that approaches Him freely?

From God's perspective, His existence in His Essence and outside His Essence are one and the same thing. The created creator of time is God the Father, Son and Holy Spirit. We might say that the two modalities are ontologically irrelevant from the point of view of Existence but also, and simultaneously, ontologically relevant from the perspective of Essence. This is, again, only an analogical way of attempting to grasp the relationship between eternity and time and existence and essence. This is also why time is important. God's existence, outside Himself, is not an illusion or a ghostly emanation but an integral expression of His own eternal existence in different modalities. As it says in Revelation 1:8:

*"I am the Alpha and the Omega," says the Lord God, "who is and who was and who is to come, the Almighty."*

God's knowing of Himself, as the Alpha and the Omega or the beginning and the end, necessarily leads to the creation of the "energies" and, consequently, time and space which is simply God's infinite Nature, mirrored in a complex and almost organic space-time geometry expressing dimension and duration in all possible directions at once.[69] The paradox can be stated: could there ever have been a time when God did not know how and why He might be imitated? Time is what occurs or is created when God knows Himself, outside Himself, which is from eternity. In this sense, time may only have a beginning in reference to God alone.

## Reinterpreting Essence and Existence

Thomas Aquinas insisted that God and His ideas were one in the Divine Essence. God does not, at one time, have an idea about us and the universe and then, at another time, have a different idea. It is all at once in eternity. There could not be a time when God did not know why and how He might be imitated. We could also say that within God there is no necessary reason to distinguish between time and eternity. Within, so to speak, the Act of God's Existence, the knowledge of time is One with that Act, and is only *other than that Act,* outside of God's existence within His Divine Essence. There is, in this formulation (to repeat below) the hint of an immediate relationship between time and eternity, mediated by God's own Existence in two modalities. Time is infinitely expanded in both directions and englobed by God's own knowledge of Himself both as He is and

---

[69] There is an enormous amount of theological literature on this subject but to state that the matter has been resolved to the satisfaction of all theologians would likely be premature.

as he might be known. What is St. Thomas Aquinas's notion of participation but a kind of virtual reality whereby what is eternal shares something of itself with what is created? What is created is a plurality[70] consisting of God and man.

*There could not be a time when God, in His own eternity, did not know why and how He might be imitated and this knowledge represents a plurality of consciousness in infinite time—God's and ours. This plurality of consciousness, however it may be differentiated, is concomitant with the Divine Energies.*

This assertion could be viewed analogously (and this is a very broad analogy) as a virtual reality embedded in a space-time similar to a Mobius strip, also known as a twisted cylinder, in which a two dimensional object (usually a strip of paper) rotates through three dimensional space to turn back on itself. God's knowledge of Himself necessarily includes all of the ways in which He could be known and like a Mobius strip, simultaneously reveals and hides itself, in the way that any beginning point of the strip is also the end of the strip. The relationship of time and eternity, when compared to a Mobius strip, might also be predicated of essence and Existence. They are two sides of some original unity. The side you see is based on whether you are looking at the starting point as the beginning or the end point. Eternity makes no conceptual sense unless it can be contrasted with time. Likewise non-contingent Existence would have no contrast or no external intelligibility without the contingency of essence. Time as the expression of

---

[70] I am indebted to Fr. Mark Byrne for clarifying this idea in a marvelous sermon he gave in May of 2014 at the Christendom college chapel.

something completely eternal and radically non-contingent[71] would, in fact, be already contained, as a mirrored possibility, within this radical non-contingency.

Physicist David Bohm hypothesized that there are two kinds of order in nature: what he called the *explicate order* (the stuff that we see) and a hidden *implicate order*. The implicate order for Bohm was a way of acknowledging how quantum mechanics reveals a hidden order where our world is influenced by *the whole of all possible states*. God, in knowing Himself in all the ways in which he might be imitated, could be said to be the sum of all possible states from the perspective of eternity. The implicate order is could be used analogically to help illustrate the actus essendi of Aquinas.

The *actus essendi* of Aquinas, if I understand it correctly, is indicative of two modes of being: Being as the uncreated Divine Essence and being *as it is given to and participated in* by creatures. The mystery of the essential order, in Thomism, is that essence, or what is sometimes called form, and the contingent existence that maintains that essence, as form, are *both* given by God in creation but God Himself undergoes no change in the process. He remains completely free of any sort of contingency or process related to contingency. In other words, the Christian God is not bound to any "system" or the explicate order but to His own Essence and that is not a system, as we might conceive of it, but rather the ultimate freedom and radical non-contingency of Existence Itself—the "I am who am"

---

[71] Wilhelmson, Frederick, *The Paradoxical Structure of Existence,* University of Dallas Press, 1970

of the Old Testament and the implicate ordering principle of the universe. Thomas Aquinas' understanding of the distinction, as noted below, is the essential position of Thomistic academia.

*"The perfection of each thing, as understood by God, is the cause of the individual things found in nature. Each individual horse shares in (is an effect of) the necessary perfection of "horseness" as understood by God while it simultaneously contains the accidental properties that make it this horse instead of any other horse. However, just because the horse is caused by the perfection, the horse does not participate in the perfection. The individual horse is ontologically distinct from the perfection even though it is caused by the perfection. The effect shares in the cause, but the effect is not the same as the cause. Furthermore, the cause can exist without the effect, but the effect is dependent upon and necessarily subsequent to the cause. Since the relationship between the perfection in God and the created thing is a relationship of cause and effect, Aquinas demonstrate[s] that all things have a beginning."* [72]

As a relevant aside, we do not have the complete written works of Aristotle to consult but there is clear evidence that Aristotle's concept of the Unmoved Mover, as causing all things to imitate Him both in terms of goodness and excellence, provided Aquinas with the basis for his notion of participation. Aristotle's notion of the soul as being: "the first act of a thing having life potential" suggests that all contingent acts are caused in some mysterious way by the Unmoved Mover. The twin notions of contingency and/or imitation have, in both Aristotle and Aquinas, their conceptual point of origin in God.

---

[72] Shelley, Jonathon; *God's Nature and Relation to Creation*, page 2. Source Academia.edu

The beautiful perspective of St. Thomas, which preserves the absolute independence of God, has some of the elements of a one-way street, which is rectified to some degree by the notion of participation.

*The problem, if it could be stated from a more modern perspective, is that the kind of change represented by creation, through an Unmoved Mover, is completely off the charts of our present understanding of space and time and cannot be grasped, in entirety, by the language of essence and existence except, perhaps, to say that Infinity knowing Itself Infinitely constitutes an exponential rate of self-knowledge and creates derivative forms of existence, exponentially, within time. A similar principle seems to operative in ourselves in that self seems to mirror the exponential power of the divine more clearly and more powerfully than ego.*

The paradoxical argument put forward by the late Frederick Wilhelmson was that "something that doesn't exist causes everything else to exist."[73] It is, perhaps, better to think of existence and essence as an organic unity[74] that operates through a variety of space-time manifolds that may be accessible to some degree by science.

How can we explain, for example, these words of Jesus in the Gospel of John, 14:16 without invoking a profound and dimensionally complex relationship between time and eternity? Not only has one divine Person entered time but He is promising to send a Second Person.

---

[73]Wilhelmson, Frederick, *The Paradoxical Structure of Existence,* University of Dallas Press, 1970

[74] The Tao of Lao Tzu often comes to mind in such reflections but it lacks one thing: the revelation of Christ that God is both One and Three.

*"And I will ask the Father,
and he will give you another Advocate to be with you always,
the Spirit of truth, whom the world cannot accept,
because it neither sees nor knows him. But you know him, because he
remains with you, and will be in you."*

The goal of religion, theology, philosophy and, specifically, metaphysics over the past five thousand years has been, to put it in the broadest terms, to explore this puzzling and mysterious relationship between the uncreated and the created or, using Bohm's hypothesis analogically, the implicate and the explicate order. Does the change just occur in the created with no change occurring in God or is God somehow involved in the process as more than just the Unmoved Mover? From the classical perspective of the Christian teaching on essence and existence there is no reciprocal involvement but there appears—if we use the analogs of modern physics—to be some sort of reciprocity *via a virtual construct* that allows God to interpenetrate time so that He can be seen and understood.

Seven extraordinary and profound questions emerge from these considerations:

1. How does the implicate order affect or inform the explicate order?
2. How can we further understand, in other words, the relationship between essence and existence?
3. Is it possible to express the notion of essence/form as a quantum wave or as a *quantum projection*[75] from

---

[75] I am indebted to Fritz Blackburn for his notion of an organic universe and the concept of "quantum projection." The notion of eternal or super matter

another kind of reality that uses eternity as space-time building blocks, so to speak, rather than time?

4. Is eternal time a kind of super time?
5. If eternity uses a different kind of space-time, as a building block, is there such a thing as eternal or uncreated matter?
6. Could we describe eternal matter as some sort of super matter?
7. How can we better understand the space-time artifacts of eternity if they are constructed out of super matter?

Who could understand God in his own nature without the assistance of a construct or what might be called this invisible architecture of participation? St. Thomas refers repeatedly to the notion of participation but speaks little, to the best of my knowledge, about how this participation is actually structured in relation to time and eternity. The essential order or the world of forms indicates the bridgework but not the way in which time is administered and parsed[76] by eternity. (St. Thomas was primarily concerned with preserving the absolute primacy and freedom of God's existence from systems of thought, which might require God to be constrained to act according to something external to his own Nature.)

---

is, I believe, original to my own deliberations, although there are probably others, particularly Sri Aurobindo, who have arrived at similar formulations. I have taken a cue, so to speak, from George Cantor's Aleph numbers (each number is, itself, composed of an infinite number of numbers.)

[76] In grammar: to divide (a sentence) into grammatical parts and identify the parts and their relations to each other; to study (something) by looking at its parts...

Plato understood the forms, or what Bohm called the implicate order, to exist in the mind of God. Aristotle understood the forms to be *an act* that made something be what it is as opposed to being something else. In other words, a chair is being a chair and not a bull due to something that exists beyond just the matter of its composition. The pattern of the matter in "chair," in terms of its potential, was something *put in act* by material and formal causes and then activated by a chair maker who functions as the efficient and final cause. This is a "projection" of thought, so to speak, into matter. Aristotle identified four primary causes that are still useful today in thinking about how causality actually works.[77]

---

[77] "**The material cause** is what something is made out of. The human body of made up of cells. Wooden boxes are made up of wood. Computers are made out of transistors and other electronic components. The material cause also explains the general sort of properties of something. Wooden boxes burn because they are made out of wood. The human body needs oxygen because its cells need oxygen. Finally, the material cause can be divided into two: prime matter and proximate matter. Proximate matter is matter that has some properties, such as wood, cells and electronic components. Prime matter has no properties at all. Aristotle believed that prime matter did not exist, but was theoretically necessary.

**The formal cause** is what makes a thing one thing rather than many things. The human body is human, wooden boxes are boxes, and computers are computers. The difference between a mere collection of cells and a human body is that a human body has properties and functions that come from a particular arrangement of the right kind of cells doing the right kind of things. A mere collection of cells is not the formal cause. A human body is the formal cause. The formal cause can also be divided into two: formal cause and exemplary cause. An exemplary cause is the plan in someone's mind that gave rise to a computer. Things have either a formal cause or an exemplary cause – not both.

1. Material causality
2. Formal causality
3. Efficient causality
4. Final Causality

When we look at these types of causation today, they seem less complex and involved than the detailed explanations of modern physics. However, and as a way of understanding some of the larger patterns that exist within physics, it is entirely helpful to attempt to translate the seemingly endless details of those scientific investigations into a common set of metaphysical principles.

---

**The efficient cause** is what did that. If a ball broke a window, then the ball is the efficient cause of the window breaking. Every change is caused by an efficient cause. If your eye sees, then it sees because light from the object strikes your eyes and causes you to see what is there. Efficient causes answer the "what did that" question, but do not answer how it was done.

**The final cause** is why efficient causes do what they do and why formal causes do what they do. Why do balls break windows? The final cause says that because balls are hard and windows are brittle, they break. Why do rocks fall? Aristotle said that rocks fall because they are heavy. Air is light, therefore air rises. These are all pointing out the final cause of efficient causes. To ask for the final cause of formal causes is to ask why these things exist at all. Why do human beings exist? Aristotle says that they exist to make more human beings, because they are alive. They also exist to be happy because they are rational. Why do computers exist? They exist because people made them. They wanted to use them as tools in math, gaming and business. Why do rocks exist? They exist because the wind, sea and rain break rock formations to produce rocks. These things are also final causes."
http://simplyphilosophy.org/philosophy/classical-greek-philosophy/aristotle/the-four-causes/

Imagine Aristotle and Aquinas' essences or forms analogous to the "integral" of mathematics, which is an object that can be interpreted as an area or a generalization of area. The integral in this context is an expression of eternity with limits. Every definition of an integral is based on a particular measure or ratio. What is the ratio of essence and existence? When you look closely at metaphysics and theology you see the outlines of a non-mathematical calculus[78] seeking a more perfect expression.

## The God of Physics and Theology

Albert Einstein, who viewed existence in the space-time of four dimensions (height, width, length and time) instead of just three, concluded in his later years that the past, present, and future all exist simultaneously. Later physicists have concluded that multiple dimensions exist—as many as twenty-one.[79] Mind, spirit and soul, if they truly exist, are likely part of, or manifest

---

[78] There is a tremendous opportunity for a trained Thomistic theologian and mathematician to articulate a new and non-linear calculus showing how the essential order of the actus essendi works on the basis of limits, which might be mathematically described using the functions of infinite motion, infinite speed, and infinite space delimited by time. The concept of the **Derivative** is at the core of Calculus and modern mathematics. The definition of the derivative can be approached in two different ways. One is geometrical (as a slope of a curve) and the other one is physical (as a rate of change). Time and hyperspace are derivatives, so to speak, of the interaction between eternity and infinite time. The relationship between time and eternity, mathematically speaking, might be said to be zero.

[79] See any of the works of the physicists, Michio Kaku or Frank Wolfe, which are extremely helpful in understanding multi-dimensional theory.

through a multi-dimensional, hyperspace manifold[80] beginning with the fifth dimension. One of the reasons that we cannot see thoughts or grasp the source of our own consciousness is that self-awareness has its origin in this hyperspace manifold (HM), which is composed of vibrating superstrings[81] that exist, in a

---

[80] "In string theory and related theories such as supergravity theories, a **brane** is a physical object that generalizes the notion of a point particle to higher dimensions. For example, a point particle can be viewed as a brane of dimension zero, while a string can be viewed as a brane of dimension one. It is also possible to consider higher-dimensional branes. In dimension $p$, these are called $p$-branes. The word brane comes from the word "membrane" which refers to a two-dimensional brane. Branes are dynamical objects which can propagate through space-time according to the rules of quantum mechanics. They have mass and can have other attributes such as charge. A $p$-brane [for example] sweeps out a $(p+1)$-dimensional volume in space-time called its *world-volume*." http://en.wikipedia.org/wiki/Brane. What is fascinating is that if you look at any postulated image of a brane, it's resemblance to organic tissue is startling.

[81] "In physics, **string theory** is a theoretical framework in which the point-like particles of particle physics are replaced by one-dimensional objects called strings. String theory aims to explain all types of observed elementary particles using quantum states of these strings [vibrating simultaneously or otherwise in different dimensions]. In addition to the particles postulated by the standard model of particle physics, string theory naturally incorporates gravity and so is a candidate for a theory of everything, a self-contained mathematical model that describes all fundamental forces and forms of matter. Besides this potential role, string theory is now widely used as a theoretical tool and has shed light on many aspects of quantum field theory and quantum gravity... String theory requires the existence of extra spatial dimensions for its mathematical consistency.." Five consistent versions of string theory were developed until it was realized in the mid-1990s that they were different limits of a conjectured single 11-dimensional theory now known as M-theory." http://en.wikipedia.org/wiki/String_theory

continuum between Existence and time.[82] This multi-dimensional, hyperspace exchange, or manifold, is a direct result of God contemplating Himself, as other than Himself, and is, derivatively, part of the Divine's eternal knowledge of Itself as other than itself. Think of this manifold as being constructed of *super matter*, i.e., matter, which is bounded by eternity rather than time. Science is now coming to this point of view, sideways, by asserting that consciousness may be a state of matter like plasma, liquid, solid or gas. This represents a return of sorts to Aristotle and Aquinas' notion of form or idea as originating in the Divine Mind.

Thought of in this manner, the eternal, manifesting *formally* in super matter, englobes time in such a way, as to both deposit time in the explicate order, *as sequential* and simultaneously retain it in the implicate order as infinite *and* eternal time. Eternity itself is beyond time but its creation of the fourth dimension, or time, involves a hyperspace manifold (HM) with an incalculable number of vectors[83] cascading through all variants of space-time. These vectors, ultimately, originate and terminate in the Divine Mind, for God as Aquinas has said, is not other than His own thoughts. Einstein was moving in this same

---

[82] A multi-dimensional continuum or hyperspace manifold (HM) constructed of super matter is difficult to conceptualize. A useful metaphor, although a bit far-fetched, might be the bridge of Asgard, which linked heaven and earth in old Norse mythology.

[83] Vector: a quantity that has magnitude and direction and that is commonly represented by a directed line segment whose length represents the magnitude and whose orientation in space represents the direction.

direction. He wanted to know how the "Old One" (God) thought.

*"Einstein's belief in an undivided solid reality was clear to him, so much so that he completely rejected the separation we experience as the moment of now. He believed there is no true division between past and future, there is rather a single existence. His most descriptive testimony to this faith came when his lifelong friend Besso died. Einstein wrote a letter to Besso's family, saying that although Besso had preceded him in death it was of no consequence, "...for us physicists believe the separation between past, present, and future is only an illusion, although a convincing one." [84]*

"In fact, it may be that space must include all possibilities in order to seem empty to us. So in summary, the universe we see is just a fragment nested in a timeless (everything) whole, rather than a single material world magically arisen above some primordial nothing. All universes exist without beginning or end in the ultimate arena of time, and each moment we experience exists forever." [85]

*"Einstein was followed in time by the colorful and brilliant Richard Feynman. Feynman developed the most effective and explanatory interpretation of quantum mechanics that had yet been developed, known today as **Sum over Histories**. Just as Einstein's own Relativity Theory led Einstein to reject time, Feynman's Sum over Histories theory led him to describe time simply as a direction in space. Feynman's theory states that the probability of an event is determined by summing together all the possible histories of that event. For*

---

[84] Georban, Kevin, *Everything Forever: Learning to See Timelessness* http://everythingforever.com/einstein.htm
[85] Ibid

*example, for a particle moving from point A to B we imagine the particle traveling every possible path, curved paths, oscillating paths, squiggly paths, even backward in time and forward in time paths. Each path has an amplitude, and when summed the vast majority of all these amplitudes add up to zero, and all that remains is the comparably few histories that abide by the laws and forces of nature. Sum over histories indicates the direction of our ordinary clock time is simply a path in space which is more probable than the more exotic directions time might have taken otherwise."* [86]

Other worlds are just other directions in space, some less probable, some equally as probable as the one direction we experience. And sometimes our world represents the unlikely path. Feynman's summing of all possible histories could be described as the first timeless description of a multitude of space-time worlds all existing simultaneously. In a recent paper entitled *Cosmology from the Top Down*, Professor Stephen Hawking of Cambridge writes: "Some people make a great mystery of the multi-universe, or the Many-Worlds interpretation of quantum theory, but to me, these are just different expressions of the **Feynman path integral.**"[87] (Note that an integral is a mathematical object that can be interpreted as an area or a generalization of area based on its relationship to a number of functions. Integrals, together with derivatives as a rate of change, are the fundamental objects of calculus.)

The Feynman path integral might also be described metaphysically, as the divine energies, whereby divine consciousness, existing outside of Itself, creates a multiplicity of

---

[86] Ibid
[87] Ibid

energetic forms, which are known in all possible permutations in the Divine vision. This concept is mirrored in *dimensionally interactive cyber kinesis*, a hypothesis developed in *How to Manage Your Destructive Impulses with Cyber Kinetics: Redirect Sexual Energy and Rediscover Your More Spiritually Enlightened, Evolved Self.*[88] Dimensionally interactive cyber kinesis might be considered to be divine consciousness, paradoxically subsisting as effect, in its derivative forms. These derivative forms of the *divine energies* were known to the ancients as theophanies.

Now it should be stated at this juncture that a God Who Is His Own Existence has a great deal in common with scientific atheism and the First Law of Thermodynamics, which states simply that: *energy is neither created nor destroyed.* Arguing that God makes Himself be is, perhaps, one rung above the notion that energy is neither created nor destroyed but it is very important to look at the political and social consequences of holding to one or the other of these two different perspectives. A God *who is His own existence* leads inexorably to either the Aristotelian notion of the Unmoved Mover, an impersonal entity removed from human experience, or to a highly personal God who is involved in human affairs.

Alternatively, holding to the scientific point of view that energy is neither created nor destroyed leads, ultimately, to the kind of

---

[88] O'Reilly, Sean, *How to Manage Your Destructive Impulses with Cyber-Kinetics: Redirect Sexual Energy and Discover Your More Enlightened, Spiritually Evolved Self*; published in January 2001 by The Auriga Publishing Group and Ten Speed Press

positivism that we are currently seeing in our political and legal system. Existence, taken as a simple given or without reference to a higher context, is simply like play dough to be shaped in any way that common agreement sees fit. Existence, from this perspective, has no power to shape human moral or spiritual life except as a neutral motor force translated into various and relativistic belief systems.

It is, perhaps, an indication of how far both camps may have drifted from the truth when neither can admit to the essential similarity of the basic argument, which is in the very broadest sense that existence is not created. Existence can be assumed as a given but the failure to interrogate existence for further intelligibility is no less reprehensible on the part of atheists than it is on the part of clerics who use it as a kind of super glue to make all the bits stick together.

Orthodox Christianity insists that God is simultaneously One and yet mysteriously Three at the same time. However it should be clear that this is not, on the face of it, logically possible without adverting to paradox. It is likely not possible for there to be movement between the Three Persons of the Trinity and various exchanges of regard or affection without the element of time, divinized or otherwise. The only way to dispense with the notion of time is to pretend that it is suspended or disregarded in some way by the fundamental unity and power of the self-creating Act of Existence, which obliterates all accidents and allows distinction only by way of shadows.

*"Thomas Aquinas made a categorical distinction between eternity and forever. Eternity, he said, is timelessness; forever is endless time. The*

*former is not rooted within a temporal framework whereas the latter is. "Eternity is a now; time has a now and then." Eternity cannot be divided whereas time can be." [89] Norman Geisler and H. Wayne House described it this way: Endless time is not eternity: it is just more of time. Eternity differs in essence, not merely accidentally in quantity. Endless time is an elongation of time. More of the same thing is essentially the same thing. ...There is a crucial difference between the "now" of time and the "now" of eternity...The "now" of time moves; the "now" of eternity does not move in any way." [90]*

This is an elegant argument but one which seems overly constrained. When you inject, so to speak, infinity into time you don't just get more time, you can also get an infinite now with the notion of "then" only as a derivative or accidental function of "now". That is how It moves without moving. The distinction may seem unimportant at first glance but understanding that the function of infinity is not just to extend in a linear fashion backwards and forwards but in a geometric explosion of multi-dimensional and seemingly, almost organic time paths, changes the way we might think about eternity. A space-time constructed out of eternity rather than time, while appearing to be a contradiction in terms, allows the mind to get some purchase on the way that duration and movement might be attributed to God as He manifests in the Divine Energies.

If we accept that the Second Person of the Trinity walked upon the earth, it might make more sense to assume that everything we can and will know about God occurs in some sort of time— either now or in the presence of an eternity that is constantly

---

[89] Ibid
[90] Ibid

illuminating time. This is what is meant by considering time as an artifact of eternity within the structure of participation. Time is a manifestation of the infinite or exponential time of eternity, an integral with multi-dimensional derivatives that might be expressed in sequential, derivative terms implied by a slope. Time is a result of God, understanding Himself, as other than Himself. It is God's virtual reality and His uncreated presence in time can only manifest derivatively, i.e., in a form commensurate with time and space as we know it.

Time, from the Trinity's perspective, would seem to be accidental in the same way that whether an object is to the right or the left of a person is accidental to the object. The accident is, however, a consequence of action in the world of time. In God's timelessness, what is accidental is a consequence of his "radical otherness" in relation to what He knows outside of Himself being Himself. (I imagine this as God always being at right angles, in a higher space, to anything we might think about Him.)

The Beatific Vision, for example, is a participation in the One, the True, the Good and the Beautiful but our translation of that vision, given that we are composed beings of matter and form, will always be one that involves some sort of time. Without time there is no intelligibility for the human mind. God's intelligibility is only fully intelligible to God and He is simultaneously One in eternity ("I am who Am.") and Three in sequential time and in eternity. Three Persons with One Nature: this is a paradox of astounding proportions; it suggests that God's nature[91] can never be grasped, except by God, because it represents a kind of exponential relationship between infinite force, infinite consciousness and infinite love that is more than what we mean by the seemingly static word infinite.

God's one Nature can't be represented by any rate of exponential change or progression that we can know because there is no rate of change from the perspective of eternity. There is, however, an infinite rate of change from the perspective of time relative to God's nature. Sri Aurobindo attempted to describe this ratio between eternity and time as a dynamic and secondary consciousness he called Overmind. He described it as, "an ocean of stable lightening." God's essence might be described as being in an exponential relationship with His nature in that what He Is can never be quantified, except within time, using the idea of "essence" as an abstract referent.

There will, likely, always be a conceptual gap between God and any of the intermediary forms that He may take. This gap between the One and the Many may, in fact, be indicative of some kind of fundamental ontological difference between God as One and God as Three. It is equally appropriate to call God

---

[91] One way of visualizing God's nature is to use an example from geometry. Visualize three circles with centers. If you attempt to overlap the circles by bringing them as close together as possible, without having the centers touch, you will be describing an equilateral triangle. If you overlay the centers and the circles, you will still have the distinction of one circle with three separate centers forming a cylinder. There is a distinction only of space and location in time using this example. How a unity of Three Persons and One Nature would manifest in eternity is unthinkable. (This example is provided, in part, by Fritz Blackburn and is from his unpublished manuscript, The Cosmic Embryo.)

One as it is to call Him Three but there is a paradoxical difference, which should not be shelved as an irrelevancy. Rather it should be mined for additional meaning, as we have attempted to do, by pointing to the historical arguments for the Divine Energies. The notion of a hyperspace manifold, in this regard, is simply a continuation of the same idea in a different and more modern form.

"Oneness," as has been previously noted, is more appropriate when applied conceptually to Divine Unity and God, as a Trinity of Persons with one Nature, is more appropriate when considering the concept of multiplicity or the Many.[92] God as being Himself, knowing Himself and loving Himself in the form of the Trinity is, nonetheless, an articulation using time, as we know it, to sequentially describe something that is not sequential or linear in any way. Edward Teller was absolutely correct in asserting the importance of "emotionally understanding the exponential function," as its power can be considered a metaphor for Divine action, operating through and in, an as yet, scientifically undemonstrated hyperspace manifold. Understanding these distinctions and hypotheses, in

---

[92] A natural understanding of the Problem of Universals is [seen] as the problem of the One over Many....As I have said, philosophers are not clear about what a solution to the Problem of Universals should explain, nor about the sort of explanation such a solution should be. Usually, however, the Problem of Universals is considered to be the problem of showing how numerically different particulars can have the same properties, as when white particulars share the property of being white, hot particulars the property of being hot, square particulars the property of being square and so on." What is the Problem of Universals? Gonzalo Rodriguez-Pereya, published in Mind, 2000, 109 (434), pp. 255-273

ever more clear formulations, enables us to live more vibrantly in the light of infinity and hold back the darkness of intellectual and moral limitation.

The old argument between atheism and theology is largely dismantled if the notion of Existence as being eternally intelligible in an endless potentiating of reality is accepted as the birthright of all humanity. This is the exponential version of time and eternity—one in which the dynamic of change is itself subject to infinite change. Those who claim Existence is unintelligible might be thought of as the enemies of progress and, ultimately, of mankind. Progress requires a constant movement from unintelligibility to intelligibility, from potentiality to actuality and from scarcity to abundance. Any embrace of the notion of scarcity, when we live in a universe ruled by exponential growth, is niggardly cosmology, bad theology and ultimately, bad politics.

**The Dance between Existence and the Divine Energies**

Aquinas, the absolute master of theology, and unequaled in broadness of mind, except for and only possibly by Aristotle, deftly substituted the Holy Trinity for Aristotle's Unmoved Mover, replacing what was fundamentally faceless with Three Faces but the mystery remained. Whether the "creator" is considered a faceless Unmoved Mover or a God who is Three Persons sharing One, Divine Essence, the mediation of existence between the creator and what is created, remains an endless source of puzzlement. If God remains utterly removed from what is created except as a kind of invisible power source, being at right angles, as it were from our own consciousness, we safely retain the majesty of God but gain very little additional intelligibility outside of "just accept it" within the given formulations of Aquinas and the schoolmen.[93]

Fortunately, what is one and the same in God may be further elaborated and understood in terms of the two modes of God's existence—*in His essence and outside His essence*. This is, in fact, one way of describing the paradoxical nature of God's existence[94] or the mysterious dance between the "little" being of contingent existence and the "big" Being of God's existence in His Divine Essence. God's existence in the Divine Essence does not constitute existence, in the common sense of the word, as existing out of or within a matrix. However, His existence outside the Divine Essence (only virtually so in the actus essendi or the divine energies) provides us with a rich source of intelligibility, which can further enhance our understanding of God's Existence as Three Persons within one Divine Essence. It is no less mysterious but it is more immediately approachable and resonates with what we see in the universe around us.

---

[93] "No method in philosophy has been more unjustly condemned than that of the Scholastics. No philosophy has been more grossly misrepresented. And this is true not only of the details, but also of the most essential elements of Scholasticism. Two charges, especially, are made against the Schoolmen: First, that they confounded philosophy with theology; and second that they made reason subservient to authority. As a matter of fact, the very essence of Scholasticism is, first, its clear delimitation of the respective domains of philosophy and theology, and, second, its advocacy of the use of reason." http://www.newadvent.org/cathen/13548a.htm

[94] Wilhelmson, Frederick, *The Paradoxical Structure of Existence,* University of Dallas Press, 1970

Scientists tell us that all matter is made up of fundamental particles, which have now been broken down beyond atoms, protons, neutrinos, electrons, muons, mesons, baryons, etc., into quarks.[95] It is interesting to note that three quarks[96] make up the famous proton that sits at the center of the atomic nucleus. The famous double helix of DNA, for example, may be a direct result of the interaction between mesons, which are composed of only two quarks[97]. At some future date, this might be considered a partial metaphor for the binary nature of existence and energy, in time, and outside of time. Think of it as God's signature on the sub-atomic world and the molecules of life.

It is, perhaps, an overly obvious statement but the more we understand of God, the better we are able understand ourselves. We can see, for example, that the commonplace division of human consciousness into ego and self is resonant with the notion that we have an eternal aspect in the mind of God relating to the notion of soul and a temporal, egoistic aspect, which is our knot of personal history within time.

---

[95] Quarks and Leptons are the building blocks which build up matter, i.e., they are seen as the "elementary particles." In the present standard model, there are six "flavors" of quarks. They can successfully account for all known mesons and baryons (over 200). The most familiar baryons are the proton and neutron, which are each constructed from up and down quarks. Quarks are observed to occur only in combinations of two quarks (mesons), three quarks (baryons). [Leptons are outside the scope of this book.] http://hyperphysics.phy-astr.gsu.edu/hbase/particles/quark.html

[96]http://upload.wikimedia.org/wikipedia/commons/thumb/9/92/Quark_stru cture_proton.svg/250px- Quark_structure_proton.svg.png
[97] http://hyperphysics.phy-astr.gsu.edu/hbase/particles/quark.html

What had previously existed, only in the One perfection of the Trinity, has been shared and not just shared in the abstract but really and truly shared.[98] This sharing occurs in time; it has a beginning even if it has no end. What is created and shared is truly distinct from the uncreated Creator and what has been created and shared encompasses more theological territory than may have been adverted to. Heaven and Hell are created artifacts and the birth of Jesus Christ occurred within the artifact known as time.[99] Hell, for example, did not exist until the angels fell.

The question of whether or not Heaven and Hell exist, as described by theological aficionados of pleasure and pain, tends to become less significant when considering time and souls as englobed and maintained by eternity in the present. Heaven, as it can be experienced now, is the enjoyment of God's presence in our lives. This will only deepen or become more attenuated after life. There may well be a place of everlasting fire built out of super matter but no one in their right minds would want to stay there any longer than required. The notion that some may be required to become permanent residents of hell is a bit

---

[98] "Who through his immense love became what we are, that He might bring us to be even what He is Himself." St. Irenaeus, (Adv, Hares V. Praefatio)

[99] What Jesus means when he refers to His Father as being in heaven is, likely, a metaphor for the derivative presence of the Father in Heaven based on the divine energies. What we will see of the Father in Heaven, for example, in the Beatific Vision, is likely an expression of our own contingency, in relation to a light that produces an infinitely expanding knowledge of Existence, limited only by our ability to process that information. The Trinity is in act and that One Act does not subsist or exist out of any location.

ghoulish. While some offenses may seem unforgiveable to us, the God who stayed the hand of Abraham and spared Isaac is likely the same God who spares all of us from what we might truly deserve. As a metaphor for loss, hell like the possibility of an untimely death, is a warning, a sign of great danger.

The age-old problem of correlation versus causation illustrates the dangers of ignorance in all its many forms. When the ancients were able to predict solar eclipses and other astronomical phenomena with regularity this "foretelling" became a sign of authenticity in regards not just to these pronouncement but all prophecies made by the priests. This was a correlation of one true thing with other pronouncements that may or may not have been true. If an Aztec priest, to use another example, was offering human sacrifice and at the moment the still beating heart was pulled from the victim's chest, lightening appeared in the sky, the appearance of the lightening, which may have been entirely accidental, might be correlated positively with the sacrifice, by the priest, as a sign of approval from the gods. This is clearly, correlation being used inappropriately, in lieu of a proper understanding of causation.

We, likewise, do not understand death and because of this we assign various correlatives to the meaning of death. If someone acted badly in life we assume that they are due for punishment and if someone acts well, we assume they are due rewards of one kind or another. This kind of correlation makes rational sense as it mirrors our own sense of justice and is present in many different religions. However, there is in fact, no rational or causal proof that we will be treated after life any differently by God than we are being treated now. Pushing God's punishment of mankind off to a future date is, clearly, one way of explaining His present and sometimes apparent indifference to human events but it is a correlation that remains entirely unproven. If we are caught in wrongdoing, here on earth, we are punished but punishment is never forever, and there is little reason that it should be significantly different after life.

God seems to have very little interest in physical punishment in the here and now and His direct intervention in human affairs is, clearly, limited by some unknown or not fully understood principle of His Existence. God's punishment for evil doers, in the present and in the future, is spiritual pain. We are made to live in God's light and life. Any diminution of this life is a source of spiritual anxiety and suffering. Many of those, for example, who commit suicide feel so awful inside that the only way they can conceive of stopping the pain is to end their lives. Much of what passes for depression and anxiety today is a direct result of the loss of God's grace and/or presence. The "living water" that Jesus spoke of is an absolute truth. "He who drinks this water will have everlasting life."

The correlation of infinite reward with merit and infinite punishment with vice is an attractive idea but the reality is, more likely, that life after death will have many of the same characteristics that we experience now. Choice will not cease but the results of all actions will likely be more keenly felt and understood. God's freedom, once given to a creature, can never be withdrawn. This is not to say there will not be punishment of various sorts meted out to those whose actions were reprehensible in life but they will likely be for corrective purposes and not an expression of infinite wrath.

God is the perfect host. Having provided for all of His guests from eternity, he allows them all to come to His table. If you don't behave, you will be escorted to the front door where you will quickly discover that outside of the host's dwelling there is really very little worth having.

The Incarnation, however it may have been contained, pre-eminently, in the eternal will and infinite attributes of the Three Persons, occurred in time. Jesus Christ the man has always either existed in the eternal Trinity (and only appeared in time as an effect of eternity without any change in God) or He hasn't. If the personhood of Jesus, as both man and God, hasn't always existed within the Trinity, we are faced with the conclusion that there is a fundamental difference between the personhood of Jesus Christ the man, and Christ as the second person of the Trinity. A substantial difference between the second person of the Trinity, who assumed a human nature, and the personhood of Jesus Christ is not theologically possible, since there is no time or composition in God—unless we assert the two modalities of God's existence. There is a hint of this in Jesus' modest and yet puzzling response to the man who questioned him about what he had to do to obtain eternal life.[100]

*"Why do you call me good? No one is good except God alone."* [101]

If Jesus Christ has always existed as the eternal Son, and however this may be expressed in the language of effect, without causal change in the Divine Essence, there is the risk of a kind of neo-Docetism whereby his humanity would be merely

---

[100] The Gospel of Luke 18/18 and 18/19
[101] Ibid

an "effective" expression of His divinity in the accidental[102] manner that colors appear in objects. In other words, Jesus' divinity would so overwhelm his humanity, as to make it irrelevant. This would seem not to be the case as indicated by Jesus' cry on the cross as He was dying: "My God my God, why have you forsaken me?" If there was ever a moment that indicates a special dynamic between time and eternity, it would be this one. Clearly, Jesus as a man, in this specific instance, was not fully cognizant of the understanding that Jesus, as the Son of God from all eternity, must have had. Theologians can dance around the matter in terms of Jesus "being allowed" to experience what it was like to be separate from God but this would appear to be a theologically superficial explanation.

In order to understand the consciousness, so to speak, of Jesus Christ an analogy from human psychology may be helpful. Psychology frequently makes the distinction between self and ego. We don't experience our "selves" or our egos as being other than who we are but we can distinguish between the two in the sense that the ego contains a kind of immediacy of thought, emotion and sensation, while the self seems somehow deeper and more hidden. A true psychology understands that very word "psychology" means study of the soul, and so from

---

[102] Accidents are the modifications that substance (the composition of matter and form) undergo, but that do not change the kind of thing that each substance is. Accidents only exist when they are the accidents of some substance. Examples are colors, weight, and motion. For Aristotle there are 10 categories into which things naturally fall. They are substance, and nine accidents: Quantity, Quality, Relation, Action, Passion, Time, Place, Disposition (the arrangement of parts) and Rainment (whether a thing is dressed or armed, etc.).

the perspective of a spiritual psychology, we can say that the self is emblematic or symbolic of the deeper operations of soul. If the ego is the tip of the iceberg, then the self, not unlike the subconscious, is the larger part of our identity and the part that seems to come to the forefront of consciousness in times of difficulty.

Using the same analogy and in order to understand the divine awareness of Jesus Christ, we might say that the eternal personhood of Christ functioned in a manner similar to the way we discover the deeper depths of ourselves. In our case, we discover the semi-eternal person we are, as we contingently participate in God's existence. In Jesus' case his identity between ego and self would, likely, have functioned in a similar way with the profound difference being that Existence itself, in the eternal person of the Son, replaced the secondary act of a contingent soul. The traditionalists have stated that Jesus had both a human will and a divine will. This cannot simply be asserted without attempting to understand how having two wills might get translated by a human and divine consciousness.

Jesus' knowledge of Himself would be a blended identity of ego and self with "self" being something a little more hidden than a complete and immediate access to the Godhead. This would explain many of the more curious statements of Jesus, whereby he seems to denigrate himself or his knowledge in order to exalt the pre-eminence of God the Father. This analogy further helps us understand the notion of the mystical body of Christ, whereby all of mankind is united in a new kind of consciousness through the divine selfhood of Jesus Christ.[103]

## The Dynamic between Time and Eternity

Theologians will say that God's Divinity so perfectly respects His humanity that there is no conflict between the two. If that is the case then it may be asserted that God's relationship with time, in the two modalities of His existence, subjected Jesus to the limitations of time, irrespective of His Divine origin. This cannot simply be glossed over; it has real metaphysical, theological and scientific consequences.

*The Incarnation, life and death of Jesus Christ is, in fact, theological proof that the divine energies exist and that God can and does exist outside of the Divine essence.[104] When we say that God walked upon the earth in the person of Jesus Christ this has to mean something substantial or it means nothing.*

There is the echo of an analogy here between what we see in physics, in terms of particle and wave, and the notion of locality and non-locality. That is to say when something is observed the wave form collapses. A particle may be considered non-local without direct observation and local when observed. What this means in terms of the two modes of God's existence is that when God

---

[103] Jesus might be said to be the creator of the first spiritual applications with the institution of the sacraments. Each application or sacrament being a modality of His eternal presence that can be used to obtain grace.
[104] This can only be considered "proof" if the divinity of Christ is subscribed to.

observes Himself, as other than Himself or how He might be imitated, He goes local or exists, so to speak, outside of the Divine Essence in what we would call today a virtual manner. His very knowing of Himself in this manner is part of the act of creation. This is why creation occurred in time because God could not have observed Himself without creating the time in which such an observation could occur.

His non-local modality might be said to be, simply, Existence and his local manifestations more closely related to the essential order. There is a hint of this formulation in Henry of Ghent (1217-1293) who was the leading Augustinian theologian after the death of Thomas Aquinas. Henry made a distinction between being the divine essence and being in possession of it. Whether or not this is true, it is a useful distinction for *cataphatic* theology, which describes what God is, instead of *apophatic* theology, or the *via negativa*, which describes what God is not.

*Henry argued that the possession of the Divine Essence was a primary actuality and that the secondary actuality of considering the Divine Essence was in potency to the first.*[105]

We might say that the pre-eminence of the Father is due to his possession of the Divine Essence, while it belongs more properly to the Son to consider the Divine Essence. The union of Son and Father is perfected by the Spirit

---

[105] William Owen Duba, *Seeing God: Theology, Beatitude and Cognition in the Thirteenth Century*, page 250

who, loving the unity of their perfection, seeks to extend that order and love throughout the known universe. Given that God is, technically neither male nor female, it is not, perhaps, inappropriate to consider the Holy Spirit as a being more closely akin to what we would consider female. (Remember Genesis? *"And He made them in Their image: male and female he made them."*) The close relationship between Mary, the Mother of Jesus, and the Holy Spirit indicates that this is and will continue to be a fruitful path for Trinitarian theology.

It should be clear from Henry of Ghent's argument that for God to fully consider something other than Himself would require the element of time as He would be considering Himself from a perspective other than the Act of His own existence. This is what Henry means when he says that the consideration of the Divine Essence is *secondary* in the order of being to possessing it. It can be argued, on the other hand, that God's Existence necessarily includes all such knowledge of the permutations of created being, from the beginning to the end of time, and that no derivative or virtual form of existence is needed[106] on His part. However, the direct knowledge of Himself, *as not Himself*, would seem impossible without a derivative mode of existence outside the Divine Essence involving time.

Furthermore, the idea that we—and all of time and history, are a creative product of the modalities of God's

---

[106] This is essentially the argument of traditional Thomists.

existence is enormously clarifying—even though from God's point of view the two modalities are almost indistinguishably welded in the infinite act and power of One Existence. Perhaps it might be easier to understand this mind-numbing line of thinking by asserting that there is no effort required on God's part to exist outside of His Divine Essence, as it is part of the Act of Trinitarian Existence, from the beginning to do so. They are simply two modalities of His being united by a third modality— that of love or the Holy Spirit. The three modalities are proper to the Three Persons and together constitute the One Nature in an exponential relationship of Personhood and Love.

If it is true that God is both One and Three then it must be true to predicate both oneness and multiplicity equally, i.e., it is as true to call God One as it is to call God Three. It would be equally inappropriate, without qualification, to suggest that His "Oneness" somehow trumps His personhood or that God is more One than He is Three. It is then, in an attempt to get some sort of intellectual traction on the nature of God, appropriate to consider God as being Three Persons from our limited perspective in time and yet simultaneously to consider God, ontologically, as being the One God of ancient Egypt and the Old Testament from the point of view of eternity. This does not obviate the mystery; it simply means that multiplicity is more appropriate a characteristic of time and oneness or unity is more appropriately a characteristic of eternity. The words of an unknown, ancient Egyptian capture an eternal truth about God:

*"He is not graven in marble"*
*"He is not beheld"*
*His abode is not known"*
*"No shrine is found with painted figures of him"*
*"There is no building that can contain him"*
*"Unknown is his name in heaven"*
*"He doth not manifest his forms; vain are all representations"*
*"His commencement is from the beginning; he is the God who has existed from old time"*
*"There is no God without him"*
*"No mother bore him, no father hath begotten him"*
*"He is a god-goddess, created from himself, all gods came into existence when he began."* [107]

"The other gods, the gods of the popular mythology, [in ancient Egypt]were understood in the esoteric religion to be either personified attributes of the Deity, or parts of the nature which he had created, considered as informed and inspired by him. It is difficult in many cases to fix on the exact quality, act, or part of nature intended. No educated Egyptian conceived of the popular gods as really separate and distinct beings. All knew that there was but One God, and understood that, when worship was offered to Khem, or Kneph, or Maut, or Thoth, or Ammon, the One God was worshipped under some one of his forms or in some one of his aspects. He was every god, and thus all the gods' names

---

[107] All quotes above from: *Ancient Egypt* by George Rawlinson, M.A., print, London, 1886

were interchangeable."[108] Rawlinson's further thoughts on the matter resonate with a curious truth.

"Ancient religions descended from the original religion. The original religion of the human race is recorded most thoroughly in the Bible. But fragments of that religion entered into the ancient pagan religions, with various modifications and gradual deviations. So is it a surprise that often times, biblical principles are found in ancient texts of pagan religions? It doesn't mean the Bible was copied from these pagan texts. It means that there were indeed revelations from God to the first people. As the original human race diverged into the different regions of the earth, they carried the religion they learned from Noah. But since they soon forgot the One true God, their religion gradually deviated from the original religion. Instead of worshiping the One true God, they created various smaller gods, from the qualities of One God."[109]

God is Three, according to Christian theology, and yet also One; three Persons with One Nature. Rather than announcing the inevitability of the paradox and closing the door to further metaphysical speculation, the notion of divine energies allows us to approach the blinding reality of both God's unity and personhood in such a way as to better understand the consequences of God's relationship to time and history. The relationship between eternity and infinite time is attested to in this startlingly simple prayer.

---

108 Ibid
109 Ibid

*"Glory be to the Father and to the Son and to the Holy Spirit, as it was in the beginning, is now and ever shall be."*

The Holy Spirit, for example, appearing as tongues of flame to the apostles, is either the uncreated Holy Spirit or some derivative effect of divine perfection entering time, or is just a symbolic projection of the Holy Spirit. Likewise, the Father speaking on Mount Tabor: "This is my beloved Son in whom I am well-pleased," cannot simply be an affect/effect or an appearance in time of some sort of pre-existing script that has existed from all eternity but rather the real deal—the uncreated presence of the Father in time. (The One is perceived as Three in time.)

*Eternal and infinite time, consequently, can only enter the fourth dimension of time in some sort of derivative or virtual format. This format is what might be termed, scientifically, a hyperspace exchange or manifold (HM). This continuum is provided by Eternity in the same manner that it provides for participation in Divine life, i.e., that while mysterious to us, this hyperspace exchange probably operates according to scientific laws that are discoverable.[110]*

Infinite time or eternity could no more enter our time, in the absolute sense, than could the ocean fit into a teacup. If we think of time in the way an electrical transformer steps down energy, we discover that time is necessary to step down the full, creative force of existence. This stepping down only occurs on

---

[110] O'Reilly, Sean *How to Manage Your Destructive Impulses With Cyber Kinetics: Redirect Sexual Energy and Discover Your More Enlightened, Spiritually Evolved Self*; published jointly in January 2001 by The Auriga Publishing Group and Ten Speed Press

our side of the fence, not on God's, except to the extent that time mirrors His actions imperfectly. The divine energies then are a creation to manifest creation, an artifact of eternity, a space-time continuum that has been designed so that we can figure our way back to God.

Politics, thought of in the old Aristotelian sense, as being a way to make citizens "good and obedient to the laws" then can become a spiritual and political tool, a way of helping people live well in the light of the Divine and the natural laws that point the way to happiness.

# III

# The Imperium:

# A New Partnership

# Between God and Humanity

"In truth, O judges, while I wish to be adorned with every virtue, yet there is nothing which I can esteem more highly than being and appearing grateful. For this one virtue is not only the greatest, but is also the parent of all the other virtues."

-Cicero, *Pro Plancio* (54 B.C.)

## The Political Consequences of Belief

The political consequences of belief, as a whole, are so numerous that listing them is hardly warranted. What is important is that belief or what reductionists scrub down to as 'reflexive truth'[111] or circular relationships between cause and effect, is at least partly true to the extent that people believe in such truths. We interpret the world around us based on what we believe or don't believe. The astonishing range of arguments between those who believe in hot button issues like climate change, abortion, gay marriage and even free enterprise and those who don't are all colored by reflexive truths—regardless of whether or not they are true in the objective sense.

The Islamic fanatics who directed airplanes at the two towers of the World Trade Center clearly believed in what they were doing but for the vast majority of people, their beliefs were insane. What person in their right minds could believe that God would reward them with seventy virgins for such bad behavior? Clearly what we believe matters but in order for our beliefs to correctly mirror the reality of God's universe they must be constantly interrogated and interpreted with new information. The failure to interrogate belief leads to intellectual stagnation. There is no system, personal, political, religious or scientific that cannot be improved upon by reflecting on the meaning of reflexivity. (The written law, in particular, consists of reflexive truths and this is why it is self-referential.)

---

[111] The principle of reflexivity was perhaps first enunciated by the sociologist William Thomas (1923, 1928) as the Thomas theorem: that 'the situations that men define as true, become true for them.' [WP]

*"Reflexivity refers to circular relationships between cause and effect. A reflexive relationship is bidirectional with both the cause and the effect affecting one another in a relationship in which neither can be assigned as causes or effects. In sociology, [awareness of] reflexivity therefore comes to mean an act of self-reference where examination or action "bends back on", refers to, and affects the entity instigating the action or examination...To this extent it commonly refers to the capacity of an agent to recognize forces of socialization and alter their place in the social structure. A low level of reflexivity would result in an individual shaped largely by their environment (or 'society'). A high level of social reflexivity would be defined by an individual shaping their own norms, tastes, politics, desires, and so on. This is similar to the notion of autonomy."* [112]

The notion that God can exist in multiple modalities is not without political, social and religious consequences. Religious conservatives and the spiritually orthodox will leap to the

---

[112] [WP] http://en.wikipedia.org/wiki/Reflexivity_(social theory)
Sociologist Robert K. Merton (1948, 1949) built on the Thomas principle to define the notion of a self-fulfilling prophecy: that once a prediction or prophecy is made, actors may accommodate their behaviors and actions so that a statement that would have been false becomes true or, conversely, a statement that would have been true becomes false—as a consequence of the prediction or prophecy being made. The prophecy has a constitutive impact on the outcome or result, changing the outcome from what would otherwise have happened. Reflexivity was taken up as an issue in science in general by Karl Popper (1957), who called it the 'Oedipal effect', and more comprehensively by Nagel (1961). Reflexivity presents a problem for science because if a prediction can lead to changes in the system that the prediction is made in relation to, it becomes difficult to assess scientific hypotheses by comparing the predictions they entail with the events that actually occur. The problem is even more difficult in the social sciences. http://en.wikipedia.org/wiki/Reflexivity_(social_theory)

conclusion that such thinking leads to immanetization. This is the idea that the eschaton[113] (the final heaven-like stage of history) is being immanetized, in the pejorative sense of the phrase coined by Eric Vogel: "Don't let them immanetize the eschaton." This phrase more correctly refers to the denigration of Hegelian academics who seek constantly to reduce what is divine to some sort of exclusive expression of materiality.

Properly understood, *the eschaton is a metaphor for a continuous relationship between God's Nature and the artifact called time,* i.e., creation is not just a seven day event;[114] it too is an artifact. What this means, derivatively, is that the eschaton may not have been properly understood to begin with. The elevation of the material order to eternity is not an eschaton but rather the power of the Uncreated to remake creation in its

---

[113] In political theory and theology, to immanetize the eschaton means trying to bring about the eschaton (the final, heaven-like stage of history) in the immanent world. It has been used by conservative critics as a pejorative reference to certain utopian projects, such as socialism, communism, and transhumanism.[1] In all these contexts it means "trying to make that which belongs to the afterlife happen here and now (on Earth)" or "trying to create heaven here on Earth."
http://en.wikipedia.org/wiki/Immanentize_the_eschaton

[114] Creation: http://plato.stanford.edu/entries/creation-conservation/
The notion of continuous creation is found both in St. Thomas and in the works of various Protestant theologians. One of the issues is the distinction between God's holding of everything in existence in his will (the notion of "occasionalism") and its stand-alone, so to speak, existence in the essential order. These arguments put the cart before the horse as existence does what it does without the benefit of or limitations of before and after. We simply cannot imagine existence; we can only point to what it appears to be doing as it may be expressed in time and the essential order.

own image. It is, in fact, a *hypostasis of the third kind,*[115] a transformation of matter into something more than matter.[116] The hypostatic union,[117] the notion of Jesus being one person subsisting in two natures,[118] human and divine, can be extended to all of creation in that the eternal Word is leading all of creation back to the Father.[119] Death is not a terminus but a

---

[115] Megan L. Ferandos, *The Orthodox Teaching on God*, Athens 1985. Chapter 7, pages 423-478

[116] Sri Aurobindo referred to this in his book, *The Life Divine*, as the supramental transformation.

[117] The hypostatic union is the personal union of Jesus' two natures. Jesus has two complete natures—one fully human and one fully divine. What the doctrine of the hypostatic union teaches is that these *two natures* are united in one person in the God-man. Jesus is not two persons. He is one person with two wills with the human will being subject to the Divine will. The hypostatic union is the joining of the divine and the human in the one person of Jesus. http://www.desiringgod.org/blog/posts/what-is-the-hypostatic-union

[118] "The doctrine of *anhypostasis* [says] that the kind of humanity Jesus took in the incarnation was *impersonal*. He did not add a human person to himself when he took a fully human nature."
http://www.desiringgod.org/blog/posts/enhypostasis-what-kind-of-flesh-did-the-word-become

[119] It could be further argued, by way of speculation, that it was not possible for just the Son to Incarnate without the other two persons of the Trinity being involved. Clearly the Spirit and the Father were involved, as Mary was told in the Annunciation, by an angel that took the form of a man: "The Holy Ghost shall come upon you and the power of the Most High shall overshadow you." (Luke 1:26-38). This is the virtual involvement of the Trinity, in time, whether by effect from all eternity or by way of the divine energies. It is precisely for this reason that Mary and the Holy Spirit have been closely linked. Mary is, as was suggested by no less than Saint Maxmillian Kolbe, an almost quasi-incarnation of the Holy Spirit. The mission

gateway into a new kind of union that involves Jesus as Lord of the entire natural order.

The notion of the eschaton is a before and after concept that does not adequately take into account that there is no before and after in eternity.[120] (God, for example, was not waiting to create us and is not waiting for us to die.) Creation from our perspective looks much more like aveternity[121] than anything else but from God's perspective there is no beginning. Everything that occurs in creation is an effect produced by an Act that does not change and that is also not limited in any way except by its own dynamic, which includes the perfection of all things and simultaneously doesn't include them from before the beginning of time. This is a paradox that really cannot be clarified unless we are able to theologically assert the dual modality of God's Existence in both time and eternity.

The idea that God simply makes all things be without any kind of movement is difficult to understand, almost magical, but when we step back from the concept and reflect on the notion that all God has to create is one, and just one, fundamental thing it becomes possible to get a handle on the notion of creation without movement. Whether this fundamental thing is being,

---

of the Son was to Incarnate. The mission of the Spirit is to uplift Mary as co-Redemptrix of the universe and mother of us all. It is the Father who sustains all of creation, including heaven and earth through the divine energies.

[120] http://philosophy.ucf.edu/fpr/files/10_1/brenner.pdf
[121] Aveternal means "having a beginning in time but continuing to exist forever."

the contingent form of existence of all things, substance,[122] energy or some sort of super matter, it is likely only one thing that is created.

---

[122] In addition to the primary mode of being, *substance*, all things have secondary modes of beings called *accidents*. Accidents are those things that allow us to imagine a being or thing. Accidents *inhere* in a substance and give it physicality. Aristotle defined ten categories of being which allow us to answer the question, "what is a being or thing composed of?" http://www.saintaquinas.com/primer.html

**The Ten Categories of Being**

1. **Substance**—substance is the primary mode of being and defines what a thing is. Substance is the foundation of reality and cannot be pictured in the mind without also picturing the accidents that inhere in the substance. The remaining categories of being are *accidents*: secondary modes of being.
2. **Quantity**—quantity allows us to define the parts in a substance. For example, a tabby cat has two ears, two eyes and a multitude of atoms and genetic material.
3. **Quality**—quality is a descriptive term such as, the softness and brown color of a tabby cat.
4. **Relation**—relation identifies the relative state between two objects. For example, that tabby cat has the same color fur as the Angolan cat.
5. **Action**—the action of the subject is also an accident. Action does not necessarily imply motion or change. For example, "the tabby cat is sitting still" is a valid action accident of the cat.
6. **Passion**—in the philosophic sense, passion is defined as change. For example, we can say that the aging process of the tabby cat is a passion.
7. **Location**—location is also an accident. For example, we could say that an accident of the tabby cat is that it is sitting on top of the sofa.

"Aristotle believed that when we ask the question "what is a thing composed of?" or "what is the nature of a being or thing?" the answer lies in the *substance* of that thing. *Substance* is a philosophic term that is defined as the primary mode of being. All things are composed of substance, which is a composition of matter and form. Therefore, the basis of reality lies in matter and the patterns we are calling form. Atoms and other particles are real, yet they are only parts of a greater whole. This is why substance is called the primary mode of being. The quantum world of physics is simply substance (matter and form) in a larger and more dynamic pattern than the ancients were able to postulate but they came very close to understanding the nature of reality in a way that science has yet to come to grips with. The patterns of quantum interaction are governed by a complex set of forms, which are in turn, governed by the Divine Ideas. These "Ideas" are already in derivative format, due to God's knowing Himself, Outside Himself.

"Now, it is important to realize that substance is not [just] an imaginative concept, it is a rational concept. This means that we can't picture what a substance is in our imagination; rather we must use rationality and logic to understand it."[123] Obviously,

---

8. **Posture**—posture identifies the spatial orientation of the subject. For example, we can say the tabby cat is sitting with all four feet on the floor and its tail is in motion.
9. **Temporality**—temporality is the affectation of time on the subject. For example, the tabby cat is seven years old.
10. **State**—state seems to imply change in the subject which allows us to identify it from other subjects. For example, the tabby cat currently has both eyes closed and is falling asleep.

[123] http://www.saintaquinas.com/primer.html

the notion of substance is a little hard to take when a vast plethora of fundamental particles have been observed by physicists but the notion of substance points to a fundamental underlying reality or set of patterns that is at the heart of all things. The fundamental difference between created and uncreated, or matter and super matter must manifest itself in terms of that which makes it different, namely time and space in terms of some sort of manifold. Super matter only makes sense in the context of super time.

God's knowing of Himself, Outside Himself, is a creative act which simultaneously produces super space and super time, which we would refer to today as hyperspace or multi-dimensionality. Multi-dimensionality, in other words, produces our four dimensional space-time, as a kind of derivative of God's self-knowledge. It is, however, and for God almost accidental in relation to His eternal nature as it adds nothing to God. It does, however, add something to us; namely our existence.

When we understand, in more scientific terms, what can now only be postulated metaphysically, we will likely have the key to the gates of creation. Given that the world we see around us is not simply a magic show without scientific causes and effects that can be demonstrated, the notion of intermediary states between the uncreated and the created is not an irrational proposition. If what God creates is be-ing or a kind of secondary existence contingent upon His own Existence then surely we should be able obtain some evidence of this from secondary

---

effects. The creation of be-ing is meaningless without something that "issing" the nature of being. Ascribing existence to all things that actually are only indicates that the notion of substance, like being itself, is a placeholder for something that has never been fully understood. Super matter, like substance, is an attempt to garner a greater understanding of the real relationship between heaven and earth.

Could it have been that God created Himself as a kind of third-party administrator or Demiurge in the virtual reality that is our space-time? We can speculate that If God wanted to create Himself in a version that could be knowable by beings, other than Himself, He would, likely, have to re-create His own Existence in a secondary format. Regardless, the *articulation* of creation probably occurs in a way that involves the secondary and contingent formation of a ratio[124] or multi-dimensional medium of exchange using the Divine energies. This is super space-time, in all its forms, which along with super matter (built with eternity instead of time) are likely, the two primary artifacts of eternity. All we can do is accept our conceptual limitations in this regard and acknowledge that no such limitations apply to God. It is important, however, to understand that how we conceive of Existence and our relationship with it is, literally, a matter of life and death.

*A political system that understands that creation is a present summons and not an archaeological event will help set mankind on the path to a new relationship with God.*

---

[124] Ratio defined as: Relation in degree or number between two similar things

The divine energies are exerting a constant force, so to speak, on the earth to transform what is limited into something unlimited. Creation is an on-going process[125] for the entire essential order. What it is to the Three Persons in One God is entirely unknown except, perhaps, as a concatenation of endless existence, consciousness and joy, which the Hindus call, *Satchitananda.*[126] This is only the temporal hint of a vastness that is that is outside the uncreated reality of God. What it is in Itself is beyond comprehension.

If we think about the *divine energies* as being the real power[127] behind what we are currently calling evolution, then a great many pieces of the picture puzzle of human existence are suddenly illuminated. Creation is continuous, as is Existence; it never started, it never stopped and it never will end. We are bathed in the rose red light of an eternal temple from the time we are born until we die. It is the immortal fire, which lights the world, and we go from light to greater light in virtue, or from darkness to greater darkness in vice.

God made us His children from the beginning and came back in the person of His Son to remind us that He made us His children—not in the hokey sense of tent-revival Protestantism

---

[125]http://www.apuritansmind.com/the-christian-walk/the-doctrine-of-continuous-creation-by-dr-c-matthew-mcmahon/

[126](The Hindu formulation of the Trinity: *Satchitananda.* "Sat" means existence, "chit" means consciousness and "ananda" is bliss or joy.)

[127] This is a notion that has found expression in the works of Teilhard de Chardin and Sri Aurobindo. The latter's notion of the descent of a supramental force/consciousness into matter is, essentially, a modern reworking of the concept of divine energies.

or the tedious repetition of prelates who have ceased to believe in anything else but Sunday football and cocktails—but really and truly His children. Our likeness to God is such that what we do to each other we also do to Him. This points to a truth so profound that we can only stand in wonder before it. We live and have our being continuously in the glory of creation, in the Act of Existence that has no beginning and has no end. The creative power and love of God does not change; it has never changed. We change—that is where we live—in the light of an infinite transformation. There is a hint of this change brought about by the Incarnation and Resurrection when Jesus says:

> *"I will not leave you orphans; I will come to you.*
> *In a little while the world will no longer see me,*
> *but you will see me, because I live and you will live.*
> *On that day you will realize that I am in my Father*
> *and you are in me and I in you."* —John 14/18

Our history is like the childhood of gods who have a psychological disorder. Until we realize the extent of the gift we have been given, as creators and participants in Divine Life, we will continue to engage in a wearying cycle between fear of the unknown and the hope that if we just repeat the right words and thoughts, and insist that everyone else repeat the same words and thoughts, we will get it right. There is no reward for doing the right thing except the right thing. It is its own reward. More importantly, until we realize that we must create with the same Spirit that created us, we will never have peace on earth.

> *"Valor fares starward, fear, to the realm of death."*
> -Seneca, *Hercules Oetaeus*

## The Imperium: A New Partnership between God and Humanity

It is, consequently, thought-provoking and refreshing to think about an institution that might guarantee both the eternal truths of religion and the truths of the relative order that we live in. This is the ultimate promise of the Imperium: a political structure that really works. One that is truly "of, by and for the people" by recognizing both the authority of God and the authority of man. The Declaration of Independence and the Constitution acknowledge the Creator primarily by way of assumption. A more direct approach would seem to be needed for the present age. The issue cannot be pussy-footed around any longer.

Organized religion, when it oversteps the bounds of common sense and voluntary association, needs to be reined-in by civic authority as much as civic authority needs to be informed by religious and spiritual values. How can a new synthesis of politics and religion better serve mankind without engaging in the morally and spiritually unprofitable separation of Church and State? How can the energy of the antithesis between religion and politics be turned into a creative endeavor?[128] The Spirit may provide the key for a creative solution to the age-old struggle between politics and religion.

*"The higher judge is the universal and absolute Spirit alone—the World-Spirit...The relation of one particular State to another presents, on the largest possible scale, the most shifting play of individual passions, interests, aims, talents, virtues, power, injustice, vice, and*

---

[128] The Father desires worshippers in truth and spirit. This is no less true of individuals than it is of institutions.

*mere external chance...Out of this dialectic rises the universal Spirit, the unlimited World-Spirit, pronouncing its judgment—and its judgment is the highest—upon the Nations of the World's History; for the History of the World is the World's court of justice."* [129]

—*Schiller*

The universal World Spirit, as conceived by Schiller, might be better thought of as a metaphor for God's continuous and creative action on and within human history. The Spirit, as mediator between the two modes of God's existence, or between Father and Son, would not likely support reinstituting the failure of political institutions, so interpenetrated by religious or theological authority, as to create a fascist neo-papal political order or an Islamic-style, authoritarian state. Neither would the Spirit desire the other side of the coin of intolerance—the pie-on-earth philosophy of Karl Marx's atheistic Communism—which is no less demanding than any religion. Communism proved itself to be a moral and social disaster by imagining that Spirit was simply part of history, a universal spirit, without transcendental aspects. We have had a preview of the wrong way to go, so there is no point in repeating the old errors. Nonetheless, the possibility of repeating the errors of history is a reality based on the nature of human freedom. God allows us to make a mess over and over again until we get it.

The transcendental aspects of what Schiller called Absolute Spirit can only be truly understood in the light of the Christian

---

[129] http://www.gutenberg.org/files/6798/6798-h/6798-h.htm

*transcendentals*; namely the One, the True, the Good and the Beautiful. Without the mirror of the transcendentals, sharing with us the true face of God, humanity descends into the darkness of Hegel's dialectical materialism, which is little more than a cosmic meat grinder for both God and man.

The toll of human suffering in North Korea and sub-Saharan Africa, for example, would never be tolerated in a world infused with transcendental spiritual and moral values. How can we take the moral and spiritual power of religion and use it to guarantee the power and authority of the individual in such a way as to create desirable social and political institutions that actually work? How can we make such an institution morally, psychologically and politically attractive? How can such an institution be made to behave, in the words of Cicero:

*"...like a trustee, morally obliged to serve society"?*

On the one hand it can be argued that this is what the Declaration of Independence and the Constitution of the United States are supposed to guarantee but on the other it can be argued that a more comprehensive document and institution that embody these same beliefs seem likely to be required, in the near future, for a world that does not entirely share in the Christian vision. This is also why a concept like the "divine energies" is politically relevant. How we view our relationship with God and how that relationship is expressed politically is at the very root of what makes laws good or evil. Hinduism, for example, would find this notion entirely consonant with many of its theological teachings going back thousands of years. The monotheism of Judaism and Islam, likewise, might also find

117

some comfort and purchase in the notion of a transcendent God utterly beyond and yet equivalent to the local configuration of Father, Son and Holy Spirit. In other words, metaphysics and theology might be used as a tool for political reconciliation, instead of division.

The Founding Fathers, from the American perspective, assumed Christian or at least Deist values in crafting the legal documents of our nation. As Thomas Jefferson noted:

*"Man has been subjected by his Creator to the moral law, of which his feelings, or conscience as it is sometimes called, are the evidence with which his Creator has furnished him....The moral duties which exist between individual and individual in a state of nature, accompany them into a state of society. Their Maker not having released them from those duties on their forming themselves into a nation."* [130]

Our legal system is presently re-imagining the Declaration of Independence and the Constitution, based on legal positivism, without the assumed moral and intellectual values of the Founding Fathers. This is a dangerous and foolish enterprise as the ultimate result will likely be a return to the old immoralities and cruelties of the pagan world. The words of one section of Alan's Ginsberg's famous poem, *Howl*, come to mind when imagining a world run on the model of positivism without recourse to spiritual and moral values.

---

[130] Natural Law: http://www.nccs.net/natural-law-the-ultimate-source-of-constitutional-law.php

*"What sphinx of cement and aluminum bashed open their skulls and ate up their brains and imagination? Moloch! Solitude! Filth! Ugliness! Ash cans and unobtainable dollars! Children screaming under the stairways! Boys sobbing in armies! Old men weeping in the parks! Moloch! Moloch! Nightmare of Moloch! Moloch the loveless! Mental Moloch! Moloch the heavy judger of men! Moloch the incomprehensible prison! Moloch the cross bone, soulless jailhouse and Congress of sorrows! Moloch whose buildings are judgment! Moloch the vast stone of war! Moloch the stunned governments! Moloch whose mind is pure machinery! Moloch whose blood is running money! Moloch whose fingers are ten armies! Moloch whose breast is a cannibal dynamo!"*

Walter Lippmann, in his definitive work, *The Public Philosophy*,[131] published in 1954 noted that: "Where mass opinion dominates the government, there is a morbid derangement of the true functions of power. The derangement brings about the enfeeblement, verging on paralysis, of the capacity to govern. This breakdown in the constitutional order is the cause of the precipitate and catastrophic decline of Western society. It may, if it cannot be arrested and reversed, bring about the fall of the West." Lippmann's prophetic words are truer now than ever before. Government works best when it acts as a repository for truth, in its many forms, and creates a level playing field to reduce the undue influence of monetary and political interests at variance with the well-being of the public. A government that takes the position that there is no

---

[131] Lippmann, Walter, *The Public Philosophy*, copyright 1956 by Mentor Books, page 19

truth to be known or protected is, ultimately, slitting its own throat.

The time has come to re-imagine a world-wide Democracy based on the American vision, infused with a pre-Christian set of moral values, lying side-by-side with Christian and other religious values, in a new synthesis that takes the natural opposition of divergent belief systems and converts it into positive, forward motion. It is time to step into the human and divine authority of the Imperium. *Sol Invictus!*[132] The unconquered sun awaits us.

### The Right to Move Forward and Change What Is Not Working

The words of the Declaration of Independence attest to both our divine right and obligation to change government when it no longer serves:

*"We hold these truths to be self-evident, that all men are created equal, that they are endowed by their Creator with certain unalienable Rights, that among these are Life, Liberty and the pursuit of Happiness. That to secure these rights, Governments are instituted among Men, deriving their just powers from the consent of the governed. That whenever any Form of Government becomes destructive of these ends, it is the Right of the People to alter or to abolish it, and to institute new Government, laying its foundation on such principles and organizing its powers in such form, as to them shall seem most likely to effect their Safety and Happiness. Prudence,*

---

[132]http://penelope.uchicago.edu/~grout/encyclopaedia_roman a/calendar/invictus.html

*indeed, will dictate that Governments long established should not be changed for light and transient causes; and accordingly **all experience [has shown] that mankind are more disposed to suffer, while evils are sufferable, than to right themselves by abolishing the forms to which they are accustomed.** But when a long train of abuses and usurpations, pursuing invariably the same object evinces a design to reduce them under absolute Despotism, it is their right, it is their duty, to throw off such Government, and to provide new Guards for their future security."*

The Third Imperium may be the system of governance that will take us to the stars and into a universe with unbounded resources for all. Modeled on the American system, with significant modifications to avoid unnecessary polarization and factions, the next section outlines how the Third Imperium might take form.

## The Twenty Two Guiding Principles of the Third Imperium

(to be incorporated into a new world Constitution)

1. The Imperium accepts all beliefs, including atheism, as legitimate from the point of view of election or free choice.
2. The Imperium does not, prima facie, accept all beliefs as equal.
3. What might be considered true is distinct from, and in opposition to, what is manifestly false. The principle of non-contradiction is invoked: "A "cannot simultaneously be "B".
4. The Imperium assumes that truth exists and is not, ultimately, unknowable within the limits of human knowledge.
5. The discovery of what is "true" or real is the essential task of mankind, as falsehood and false narratives carry within them the seeds of vice and social disorder.
6. The Imperium takes as its guide a system of morality that uses the concepts of virtue and vice and assumes belief in a Supreme Being. This will be the official public philosophy of the Imperium and will be taught in all schools.
7. The Imperium will not be guided, in a definitive manner, by any form of positivism, either in

education or in governance, except in legal contracts and science, or where applicable and useful.

8. The Imperium, in the name of freedom, guarantees the right of men and women to make wrong choices, to engage in private vices to the extent allowed by law, but never to confuse what is allowed with what is good.

9. The Imperium will guard truth in all its many forms and serve the best interests of mankind through a custodial relationship with the world and its resources.

10. The Imperium will guard the validity of all voluntary religions but be limited by none.

11. Separation of Church and State may not be construed to mean separation of the state from morality.

12. Any religion asserting the right to forced conversion will be persuaded otherwise.

13. The Imperium assumes that human population growth is not an evil and that economic development is not incommensurate with respect for Nature.

14. Banking, finance and taxation must serve the development of mankind.

15. A flat tax, worldwide, of two percent will be levied. Financial parasitism and lending at interest rates above four percent is to be discouraged.

16. The right to life is an inalienable human right and may not be revoked except under medically justified circumstances, which would include rape and incest.

17. Violent crime and terrorism, in all its forms, is completely unacceptable and will be suppressed using any and all means necessary.
18. Rape and violent crime, in the first degree, against men and women will be considered a crime against humanity and will be dealt with severely.
19. The Imperium supports the notion of Democracy and one man, one vote for men and women.
20. Marriage may only be considered valid and legal between a man and woman. Civil unions may be permitted between homosexuals but should not be considered normal, except by way of defect.
21. The US Declaration of Independence and Constitution is not just a model for America, but for the world. The Imperium must be built using these documents as its foundation.
22. The Imperium wishes all association within the Imperium to be voluntary. The goal of the organization is to conduct its affairs in such an honorable and impartial way that everyone will want to participate in its affairs.

# The Legislative Structure of the Imperium

## The Eleven Houses of the Imperium with Representatives

1. The House of Science (one representative per scientific discipline)
2. The House of Religion (one representative per religion)
3. The House of Elders (method of representation to be determined)
4. The House of Leaders (method of representation to be determined)
5. The House of Law and Justice (method of representation to be determined)
6. The House of Defense (method of representation to be determined)
7. The House of Education (method of representation to be determined)
8. The House of Morality (method of representation to be determined)
9. The House of Industrial Development (one representative per industry)
10. The House of Family (method of representation to be determined)
11. The House of Finance and Banking (method of representation to be determined)

**Nine Imperial Regions with Senatorial Representation**

(Countries within regions will be considered "states" with the number of Senators to be determined by an algorithm based on population, resources and development.)

1. North America
2. Mexico and Central America
3. South America
4. Europe
5. Russia
6. Africa
7. China, Mongolia and Tibet
8. Southeast and northern Asia
9. Australia and the South Pacific

## The Principle of Voluntary Association

Two forms of voluntary association might be initially offered within the Imperium:

1. Honorary membership whereby a country continues with its sovereign form of government and observes the activities of the Imperium but does not vote.
2. Imperial citizenship whereby a country's political institutions merge with those of the Imperium congruent with full voting rights and protection within the Imperium.

3. The essential notion behind voluntary association is that if an organization is exemplary, i.e., if its principles are effective, efficient and productive of both wealth and happiness, then the majority of creative human beings will want to be part of it.

## The Executive Structure of the Imperium [133]

The eleven Houses of the Imperium and the nine regions of Senatorial representation will each select a candidate for Regent[134] and Vice Regent after public debates modeled on the American system. The division of the world into only nine regions is to encourage state alliances and federations.

A **Regent**, from the Roman *regens*, "one who reigns," is the informal or sometimes formal title given to a temporary, acting head of state in a monarchy. These Regents will be voted upon by popular, world vote and one Regent will be elected and may serve for two terms of five years each and no more. The notion of "regency" is to reinforce the notion that the office is temporary and that the Regent serves in place of the only monarch that the Imperium recognizes: the eternal, living God.

---

[133] This and the indicted legislative and judicial structures are, simply, an outline.

[134] A **regent**, from the Roman *regens* "one who reigns", is the informal or sometimes formal title given to a temporary, acting head of state in a monarchy.

As Lao Tzu notes in *The Way of Life*:

*"One who recognizes all men as members of his own body is a sound man to guard them."*

The administrative center for world voting might, initially, be in the United States. The final location of the capitol of the Third Imperium and its immense physical and legal infrastructure for world governance will be decided by a collective majority vote between Senators from the nine Imperial Regions and Representatives of the Eleven Houses. The United Nations will be disbanded as an archaic entity whose usefulness has ended.

## The Judicial Structure of the Imperium

Thirty two Judges to be selected by a computer-aided vetting process programmed to select only most qualified and excellent jurists. The process might be guided and further vetted by the following Houses: Elders, Law and Justice, Family, Morality and Industrial Development. Fidelity to the Constitution of the Imperium will be essential. Additionally, the Judiciary will continue in its traditional role of acting as a check and balance against excesses of the Legislative and Executive branches of government. Interpretation, within the Imperial Judiciary, may not be used to change the original meaning of the law—only to nuance implementation. Judges will not be appointed by the Regent although he or she may suggest names to be vetted during their term in office. The term of a judge would be for life with recalls for moral turpitude or treason.

## A First Step

One of the ways that the Imperium might be initiated could be as an on-line game or virtual world, like Second Life, whereby individuals from different countries could act as "shadow" representatives. Once the size of the game becomes sufficiently large, by encompassing enough countries and representatives, it might start to have a political impact through "shadow voting" on popular issues.

One of the primary objections to the Imperium will, of course, be the notion that the state would, for all practical purposes, be in bed with religion. However the first guiding principle of the Imperium—that of the acceptance of all beliefs, and the eighth guiding principle, the right of citizens to a libertarian range of private vices—presumably licensed drug taking, gambling, prostitution, sodomy and other bad habits with various rational constraints, is not the kind of bed organized religion will find very comfortable.

There is a profound difference between a state that recognizes virtue and vice, and a state that confabulates the two under the notion of freedom of religion, as freedom from morality. Morality is not religion; it is simply a way of restraining some of the negative tendencies of biology and aligning the human will with higher forms of moral goodness. A state that recognizes and supports moral and intellectual excellence should have little interest in legislatively supporting, or aiding and abetting vice, except in order to preserve a sufficient level of freedom to allow men and women to choose between good and evil. The toleration of vice must never be confused with moral approval, or elevating it in public opinion, so as to put it on par with moral excellence. The true art of politics, as Aristotle noted, is to make the people as good as possible. The art of statesmanship must seek both the will of the people and the mandate of heaven.

*"Beautiful life, letting anyone attend,*
*Making no distinction between left and right,*
*Feeding everyone, refusing no one,*
*Has not provided this bounty to prove how much it owns,*
*Has not fed and clad its guests with any thought of claim;*
*And because it lacks the twist*
*Of mind and body in what it has done,*
*The guile of head or hands,*
*Is not always respected by a guest.*
*Others appreciate welcome from the perfect host*
*Who, barely appearing to exist,*
*Exists the most."* [135]

Ultimately, the notion of God as "allower," within the context of what is reasonable, and not the "denier" except in areas of obvious contradiction to goodness, such as murder, theft, rape, abortion, economic exploitation, environmental degradation, and the intellectual and aesthetic infelicities of judicial activism, may help shift the focus of politics to what is positive and productive, rather than to what is negative and destructive of human life.

---

[135] Lao Tzu, *The Way of Life*, translated by Witter Bynner, Capricorn Books, NY, 1944